Greater Efficiency in the Small Office

Greater Efficiency in the Small Office

Porter Henry

Joseph L. Kish, Jr.

ADDISON-WESLEY PUBLISHING COMPANY
READING, MASSACHUSETTS · MENLO PARK, CALIFORNIA
LONDON · AMSTERDAM · DON MILLS, ONTARIO · SYDNEY

Library of Congress Cataloging in Publication Data

Henry, Porter.
Greater efficiency in the small office.

Includes index.
1. Office management. I. Kish, Joseph L. II. Title.
HF5547.H395 651.3 82-3964
ISBN 0-201-03107-8 AACR2

ISBN 0-201-03107-8
ABCDEFGHIJ-AL-898765432

Contents

Part Three
MORE EFFICIENT EQUIPMENT

Part Four
MORE EFFICIENT PEOPLE

Preface

This book is written for that jack-of-all-trades who is managing a small office. The word "small" in this case means anything from the one-person office—such as that of a writer who has to manage his or her own manuscripts, files, correspondence, and finances—up to an office of perhaps 30 or 40 people. The manager of this small office is forced to know something about everything: how to establish procedures, how to set up files, how to manage people, how to select equipment, how far to automate.

The types of offices for which this book should be useful are real estate agencies, law firms, insurance agencies, medical and dental offices, consulting firms, district sales offices, contractors, and service offices. This book attempts to give managers of such offices a bit of practical advice on virtually all phases of office management except bookkeeping and accounting, which are more specialized subjects.

For every subject covered in this book, entire books are available. Hence the present volume is what college professors call "a survey course" —a little knowledge about every aspect of office management, with the invitation to delve more deeply into whatever subjects are found to be the most important or interesting.

Although the small office may be part of a large corporation, in most cases it is the headquarters of a small business. "Small businesses," as defined by the U.S. Small Business Administration, are those with 500 or fewer employees. They play an amazingly important role in the American economy.

In most states, 80% of the business establishments have 20 employees or fewer. Yet small businesses generate almost 50% of the Gross National Product. Most of the new jobs in America are created by small businesses. One study covering a recent 7-year period revealed that 9½ million new jobs were generated during that time. Of these, 3 million were generated by government (mostly state and local) and 6½ million by the private sector.

Believe it or not, only 75,000 of these new jobs were generated by the 1,000 largest corporations in America. The remaining 6,425,000 were generated by small businesses. So any increase in efficiency or productivity in small offices is important to the prosperity and security of the nation.

The authors are indebted to Pan American World Airways and the American Society of Travel Agents for permission to use portions of a manual, written by the same authors, called "H.E.L.P.—How Efficiency Leads to Profits." We also thank the American Management Association (AMA) and Kathy Mayer, AMA Senior Program Director, for the opportunity to conduct AMA seminars on this subject and learn at first hand about the questions faced by typical office managers; Lawrence Cummings, Regional Advocate of the Small Business Administration in Syracuse, N.Y., for reading the manuscript and offering many helpful suggestions; and Porter Henry & Co. for permission to use their time sheet and modified portions of their self-study course on the appraisal interview.

Greater Efficiency in the Small Office

Part One
BACKGROUND

1
The Profit Payoff

A 10% to 15% increase in the efficiency of an office can produce a doubling of profits.

It all depends, of course, upon what kind of paperwork and processing the office is doing. But let's suppose that an office is selling $1 million a year in services of some kind and netting 10% on sales, or $100,000 (Figure 1-1). Let's further say that paperwork, communications, and other procedures are costing $500,000 a year. If these costs could be reduced by 10%, the $50,000 savings would boost profits from $100,000 to $150,000, an increase of 50%, while a 20% reduction in processing costs would double profits, from $100,000 to $200,000.

In many cases it is just not possible to cut costs by that amount; in fact, the goal in many cases is simply to minimize the constant increase in costs. But even where out-of-pocket costs cannot be reduced, if some of the staff time now being devoted to paperwork can be transferred to some profit-producing function, the effect on net profit can be the same.

It is estimated that handling forms and reports required by the United States government costs about $10 billion a year, and doing paperwork required by state and local bodies costs another $2.7 billion.

Costs of everything are increasing almost geometrically. A first-class letter that cost 3¢ about ten years ago—remember?—now costs 20¢. A pay-station phone call from Manhattan to the nearest Westchester County suburb has increased from 5¢ to 30¢. The cost of nearly everything, including capital, has tripled.

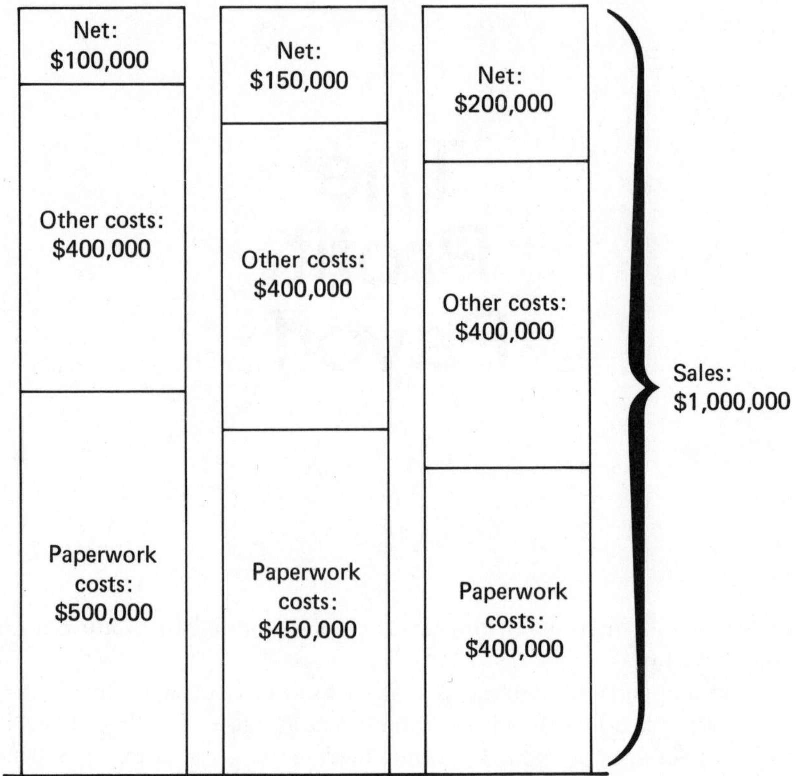

Figure 1-1
The Effect on Net Profits of a 10% and a 20% Reduction in Paperwork Costs

Improved efficiency yields benefits other than the obvious financial ones:

- Service to customers is improved.
- There is less stress and tension in the staff.
- Employees enjoy a feeling of accomplishment.
- The manager sleeps more soundly at night.

Yet many office managers are so busy trying to keep up with the increasing complexity of doing business that they cannot find the time to take a long, hard look at their present procedures and develop more effective ways of handling things. They are, as the old adage puts it, so busy chopping wood that they don't have time to sharpen their axes.

This book explains how the manager of a small or medium-sized office can take a fresh look at the office's methods and work out ways of saving time and money. It is addressed to the manager of the smaller office, since giant firms like the major insurance companies have full-time experts working on these problems. Although we will cover the role of computers, word processors, and other automated equipment, the emphasis will be on labor-saving shortcuts that can be introduced without investment in new equipment.

The next section of the book deals with the question, "How can we make ourselves more efficient with the staff and equipment we have now?" We will look at a technique called "work simplification," a systematic way of analyzing your existing procedures to eliminate unnecessary steps and produce the same results faster, more easily, and at a lower cost.

Next come chapters on how to develop better ways of handling everyday office functions: telephoning, filing, correspondence, copying, forms. We will look at office layout and discuss ways of developing your own policies and procedures manual.

What about automation? You will get a briefing on the functioning of computers and yardsticks for determining whether it would be more profitable for you to buy one, lease one, use a computer service bureau, or retain your manual methods.

But equipment and procedures are only as good as the people who use them. What motivates people? We will examine that, along with "staff utilization"—making sure that the office functions are divided among employees in the most effective way.

We will then cover salary administration; the recruiting, selection, and training of new employees; legal aspects of the wage-hour and other laws; and finally some time-tested ways of developing the skills and abilities of individual staff members.

Application of these ideas will require effort, but that effort will pay off in lower costs, greater productivity, and that satisfying feeling of being "on top of the job."

2
Basic Principles

Although this book covers many specific aspects of office efficiency—forms, filing, mail, telephones, and so on—there are certain basic principles that apply to all aspects of office efficiency. These will be covered in this chapter; later chapters will show how they apply to specific functions.

BE AWARE OF STAFF COSTS

In most offices, payroll (including the manager's salary) is one of the major costs. In a travel agency, for example, it represents 50% to 60% of all costs.

In comparing the costs of different ways of handling an office task, the key question is, "What is the cost of staff time involved in the different methods?" In considering whether to buy a new piece of equipment the question is, "What is the dollar value of the staff time it will save, and how quickly will that saving pay for the equipment?"

The basic unit we will be referring to in this book is "staff time per working minute"—and it costs more than many managers realize, especially after adding the cost of space, equipment, and other overhead items required by the employee. It will take you about 5 minutes to calculate this cost for an average employee, and it may be an eye-opener.

Table 2-1 is a form for calculating the per-minute cost of staff time. If all employees receive approximately equal salaries, you can use an average figure. If some are paid substantially more than others, work out the per-minute cost of staff time at each salary level. Run off duplicate

Table 2-1
The Per-Minute Cost of an Employee's Time

Salary costs			
Annual salary		________	
Fringe benefits:			
Pension contribution ________			
Insurance ________			
Medical ________			
Social Security ________			
Other ________			
TOTAL FRINGE BENEFITS (approximately 25%)	(*plus*)	________	
Total annual salary costs		________	(1)
Time worked			
Days worked each week × 52		________	
Subtractions:			
Holidays per year ________			
Vacation days ________			
Sick leave ________			
Meetings, training ________			
Other ________			
TOTAL DAYS OFF	(*minus*)	________	
Total days worked per year		________	(2)
Salary cost per day worked— (1) divided by (2)		________	(3)
Number of minutes worked per day (8 hours = 480 minutes)		________	(4)
Salary cost per minute worked— (3) divided by (4)		________	(5)
Overhead cost per minute worked— (5) times "multiplier" *		________	(6)
Total cost per minute worked— (5) plus (6)		________	(7)

* To determine the amount of overhead costs to allocate to each minute of an employee's time, get a "multiplier" by dividing overhead costs by salary costs. The word "overhead" here means total costs minus salary costs. Multiply the salary cost of an employee minute by this "multiplier" to get the amount of overhead costs to add to the salary cost. Example: total costs, $120,000; all salary costs, $72,000; "overhead" costs, $48,000. "Multiplier" is $48,000 divided by $72,000 equals 0.67. If an employee's salary cost is 12¢ per minute, the allocated overhead costs are 12¢ times 0.67, or about 8¢.

copies of Table 2-1 and work out a table of the per-minute cost of staff time at various salary levels.

As an example, Table 2-2 has been filled out for a hypothetical employee. Let us go through it line by line. The base salary is $12,000 per year. What is the total of other salary costs, such as Social Security taxes, pension funds, and so on? You can arrive at this figure in one of three ways:

Table 2-2
Sample Per-Minute Cost of an Employee's Time

	Salary costs			
Annual salary			$12,000	
Fringe benefits:				
Pension contribution				
Insurance				
Medical				
Social Security				
Other				
TOTAL FRINGE BENEFITS (approximately 25%)		(*plus*)	$ 3,000	
Total annual salary costs			$15,000	(1)
	Time worked			
Days worked each week × 52			260	
Subtractions:				
Holidays per year	10			
Vacation days	15			
Sick leave	5			
Meetings, training	5			
Other	5			
TOTAL DAYS OFF		(*minus*)	40	
Total days worked per year			220	(2)
Salary cost per day worked— (1) divided by (2)			$68.18	(3)
Number of minutes worked per day (8 hours = 480 minutes)			480	(4)
Salary cost per minute worked— (3) divided by (4)			14.2¢	(5)
Overhead cost per minute worked— (5) times "multiplier" *			9.5¢	(6)
Total cost per minute worked— (5) plus (6)			23.7¢	(7)

* To determine the amount of overhead costs to allocate to each minute of an employee's time, get a "multiplier" by dividing overhead costs by salary costs. The word "overhead" here means total costs minus salary costs. Multiply the salary cost of an employee minute by this "multiplier" to get the amount of overhead costs to add to the salary cost. Example: total costs, $120,000; all salary costs, $72,000; "overhead" costs, $48,000. "Multiplier" is $48,000 divided by $72,000 equals 0.67. If an employee's salary cost is 12¢ per minute, the allocated overhead costs are 12¢ times 0.67, or about 8¢.

1. You can itemize it in detail for each employee.
2. You can total up all fringe benefit costs for the entire office, divide by the total payroll, and get a ratio that you can apply to each employee. For example, if payroll totals $60,000 and fringe benefits cost $17,000, then $17,000 divided by $60,000 = 0.283, or 28.3%. For any employee, multiply his or her base salary by 0.283 to get the approximate cost of fringe benefits.
3. You can use a rough estimate of the total, such as 25% (as has been done in the example). With a base salary of $12,000 and fringe ben-

efits totaling an estimated 25% of salary costs, the fringe benefits for this employee cost about $3,000 per year.

Adding the "bare" salary cost, $12,000, to the fringe benefit cost of $3,000 gives a total of $15,000 in salary costs for this individual.

Now we figure the salary costs (without allocating overhead costs) for each working minute of this employee. The employee works five days a week, multiplied by 52 for a total of 260 days a year before subtracting nonworking days. Subtracting the 40 listed nonworking days leaves 220 days worked.

The total salary cost of $15,000 (line 1) divided by 220 days gives a salary cost of $68.18 per day. Dividing this by the 480 minutes worked per day gives us a salary cost of $0.142, or 14.2¢ per minute.

But what about overhead costs? To enable this employee to work, the office must provide floor space, a desk, heat, light, and equipment. Strictly speaking, some of these are operating expenses rather than overhead expenses; but for purposes of calculating what this employee costs us per minute, we will lump under the term "overhead" all expenses other than salaries and related fringe benefits.

To calculate the amount of overhead to allocate to each employee, we work out a "multiplier" by dividing overhead (meaning "all other") costs by salary costs. For example, if salary costs are $72,000 and all other costs are $48,000, the multiplier is 0.67. For every $1 of salary costs we have to add 67¢ to cover overhead costs.

Since we defined "overhead" as all costs other than salaries and fringes, the formula becomes:

$$\frac{\text{total costs minus salary costs}}{\text{salary costs}} = \text{multiplier}$$

On line 6 we multiplied the bare salary cost per minute by the multiplier, 0.67, to get 9.5¢ in allocated overhead. Adding that to the 14.2¢ in salary costs gives us a total cost of 23.7¢ per minute for this employee.

THE "LOWEST-PAID EMPLOYEE" PRINCIPLE

Another basic principle of office efficiency is that every task should be performed by the lowest-paid employee capable of performing that task. It does not make sense to have the morning's mail opened and sorted by someone whose total cost is 20¢ per minute if the job can be done by someone costing 10¢ per minute.

Similarly, unimportant tasks should not be handled by important people. A staff member who is good at selling or maintaining customer relations should not be required to handle paperwork if it can be designated to a less talented, less experienced, and lower-cost employee.

THE "DO-IT-YOUR-WAY" PRINCIPLE

Unless your office is part of a nationwide organization that has standardized forms, equipment, and procedures, there is no single established, proven, "right" way to do anything. What you file and how you file it, what you keep and what you discard, what each employee keeps in his or her individual desk—all these are questions that you must work out for yourself.

This book cannot hand you any ready-made answers, but it can give you the procedures for working out the answers that are best for you. In other words, this book will give you a system for improving systems, a procedure for streamlining your own procedures.

THE "FRESH LOOK" PRINCIPLE

No matter what aspect of your office operation you set out to improve, the important first step usually is to "take a fresh look" at what you are now doing and the ways you are doing it.

There are various systematic ways of taking this new look. For example:

- To work out better ways of handling outgoing mail, you first make an inventory of the types of mail you send out and the quantities of each type.
- To hold down telephone costs, you make a check of what kinds of calls are being made, by whom, and to whom.
- To simplify some routine office procedure, you first analyze your existing procedure using the "work simplification" charts described in Chapter 5.

Even if you tackle some office function not mentioned in this book, you should be able to use the "survey" or "inventory" methods it describes to analyze your present ways of doing things so that you can work out better ways.

YOU SAVE MINUTES, NOT HOURS

Except in very unusual cases, an improvement in office efficiency is not going to enable you to lay off 20%, or 15%, or even 10% of your existing staff.

The methods covered in this book will usually enable each employee to save a few minutes here and a few minutes there. If these retrieved minutes are merely wasted, the increase in efficiency will not increase profits. The important question is, "How can each staff member use these newly created minutes to do something productive, something that adds to the income or output of the office?"

For example, if an employee has 15 extra minutes a day, can they be spent in making one personal sales call or service call, or several telephone contacts with customers and prospects? Can the new time be devoted to something that will give the office more publicity, greater community acceptance, better customer service?

Part Two

MORE EFFICIENT PROCEDURES

3

Managing Your Own Time

"Where on earth am I ever going to find the time to try out some of these ideas?"

That may well be your reaction as you read the rest of this book. If you are managing an office, or some part of an office, the demands on your time are greater than the supply of it. There is just not enough time to do all the things you would like to do.

Furthermore, the pressure is always on the immediate output of your operation, not on the analysis of the procedures that produce that output. In a law office the pressure is on getting the briefs written, the contracts drawn, the trial preparations completed. In any kind of sales office the pressure is on making those calls, getting those sales, handling those orders. In an engineering, contracting, or architectural office the drive is to land the contract and then to complete it. In a publications office it is the constant pressure of deadlines.

If your office is not one of those described above, take a minute to ask yourself: "What *is* the output we concentrate on?"

Whatever type of office you manage, the problem to be addressed in this chapter is, "How can you keep up the output while simultaneously finding time to adjust the processes that produce the output?" In other words, "How can you find time to examine and repair the pipeline when the principal function is to keep things moving through the pipeline?"

In short, how does the manager manage his or her own time?

KNOW WHERE YOUR TIME GOES

Time is something like money. We all know of two families who have approximately the same income, yet one family lives comfortably, while the other is always scraping, borrowing, and living on the verge of financial collapse.

We all have the same amount of time, yet some people manage to accomplish everything comfortably within that time, while others are always frantically scurrying around to keep up with their assignments. As the old Pennsylvania Dutch proverb puts it, "The hurrieder they work, the behinder they get."

People who do not manage money wisely make three mistakes:

1. They do not know where their money goes.
2. They spend it as if the supply were unlimited; they do not realize its scarcity and value.
3. They do not budget and control their expenses.

Similarly, with time management: most people do not know where their time really goes, they spend time as if they had an unlimited amount of it, and they do not budget and control their use of time.

The logical way to begin managing your own time more efficiently is to find out exactly where your time is going. It is not good enough to estimate what portion of your time is being absorbed by your various functions; your estimate will be inaccurate. The tasks you dislike seem to take more time than they really do; on the other hand, you tend to spend too much time on chores you like to do, misleading yourself into believing that they are taking up less time than they really are.

The way to analyze your present expenditure of time is to keep a log of your time for a typical week or two. Make up a "time ladder" like that shown in Figure 3-1. Use it to keep track of your time in 15-minute segments. Chances are that in any given 15 minutes you will do several different things, but ask yourself what you were doing during *most* of that 15-minute interval and enter it in the appropriate box.

To save time, use a set of symbols for frequently performed tasks. Do not try to use the code in Figure 3-2; that's just an example. In the example:

- Te means telephone conversation, and
- TeC means telephone conversation with customer,
- TeS means telephone conversation with suppliers,
- TeA means telephone conversation with associates,
- TeP refers to personal phone conversations, and
- TeO means "other" phone conversations.

TIME LOG FOR WEEK OF ______________________

	MON.	TUES.	WED.	THURS.	FRI.	SAT/SUN.
8:30-8:45						
8:45-9:00						
9:00-9:15						
9:15-9:30						
9:30-9:45						
9:45-10:00						
10:00-10:15						
10:15-10:30						
10:30-10:45						
10:45-11:00						
11:00-11:15						
11:15-11:30						
11:30-11:45						
11:45-12:00						
12:00-12:15						
12:15-12:30						
12:30-12:45						
12:45-1:00						
1:00-1:15						
1:15-1:30						
1:30-1:45						
1:45-2:00						
2:00-2:15						
2:15-2:30						
2:30-2:45						
2:45-3:00						
3:00-3:15						
3:15-3:30						
3:30-3:45						
3:45-4:00						
4:00-4:15						
4:15-4:30						
4:30-4:45						
4:45-5:00						
5:00-5:15						
5:15-5:30						
evening						

Figure 3-1
A "Time Ladder"

TeC: telephone, customers
TeS: telephone, suppliers
TeA: telephone, associations
TeP: telephone, personal
TeO: telephone, other

ReC: reading correspondence
ReR: reading reports
ReP: reading publications
ReO: reading, other

FiR: finance, receivables
FiP: finance, payables
FiB: budget
FiS: statements

CvC: conversation, customers
CvS: conversation, suppliers
CvE: conversations, employees
CvO: conversations, others

WrR: writing reports
WrC: writing correspondence
WrP: writing promotional materials

Figure 3-2
Example of Quick "Code" of Activities

The other symbols are self-explanatory. Make up your own set of symbols, appropriate for your own work.

Your analysis will be more useful to you if you subdivide your functions into very specific tasks—not just "paperwork," for example, but "analyzing sales reports," "preparing daily recap," "preparing weekly report," and so on.

You are not expected to fill in a box at the end of each 15 minutes; however, be sure to update your log every hour or so. If you wait until noon to fill in the morning log, you will find that you cannot possibly remember exactly what you were doing between 10:00 and 10:30. If you do not accurately know what you were doing with your time 2 hours ago, consider how inaccurate your estimate would be if you tried to say where your time went for an entire week!

Table 3-1
Summary of Weekly Activities

Activity	*Total Minutes*	*% of Total*
Telephone	412	15.1
Correspondence	280	10.3
Sales calls	492	18.1
Handling complaints	131	4.8
Planning	25	9.9
Reading trade publications	185	6.8
Writing proposals	481	17.1
Reading company reports	92	3.4
Writing reports	191	7.0
Purchasing	23	1.0
Misc. administration	264	9.7
Industry meetings	141	5.2
Totals	2,717	100.00

At the end of the week, tabulate your time usage, as shown in Table 3-1, by listing all the functions you performed and, opposite each one, entering the total number of minutes you spent during the week on that function.

Now take a hard look at the way in which you allocated your time. Ask yourself:

1. What functions are taking too much time?
2. Which ones should be getting more time?
3. Which ones did I undertake on my own volition, and which were forced upon me by others?

ESTABLISH PRIORITIES

The next step toward more efficient management of your own time is to carefully determine the relative importance of every function you perform.

We are guided here by what is sometimes called "the Pareto principle," after the Italian economist and sociologist, Vilfredo Pareto. He pointed out that in any collection of a variety of objects, there are a few very important ones and a great many unimportant ones.

The principle of "the important few and the unimportant many" was further developed by the American industrial engineer, J. M. Juran. He found that for most collections the top 15% account for 65% of the results. The fastest-moving 15% of items carried in a warehouse account for 65% of total sales; the biggest 15% of customers produce 65% of the business; 15% of the city blocks in high-crime areas produce 65% of all the crimes in the city.

Taking customers as an example (Figure 3-3), Juran found that the top 15% of all customers—we call them "A" customers—are responsible for 65% of total sales. The next 20% of the customers, the "B" customers, produce 20% of total sales; and the bottom 65% of the customers, the little ones, generate only 15% of total sales.

The application of this principle to the topic of time management is this: If you list all the specific functions you perform and rank them in order of importance,

- the top 15% are the "A" functions and account for 65% of your success or effectiveness;
- the next 20% are the "B" functions, and are responsible for 20% of your results,
- the least important 65% are the "C" functions, which altogether produce only 15% of the results.

To apply this principle, use a form like that shown in Table 3-2 to list all the functions you perform, *in order of their importance*. Then classify the top 15% as "A" functions, the next 20% as "B" functions, and the remaining 65% as "C" functions. For example, if you listed 50 functions, you will have seven or eight "A" functions (15% of 50 is 7½), ten "B" functions, and 33 or 34 "C" functions. Table 3-3 is a hypothetical example.

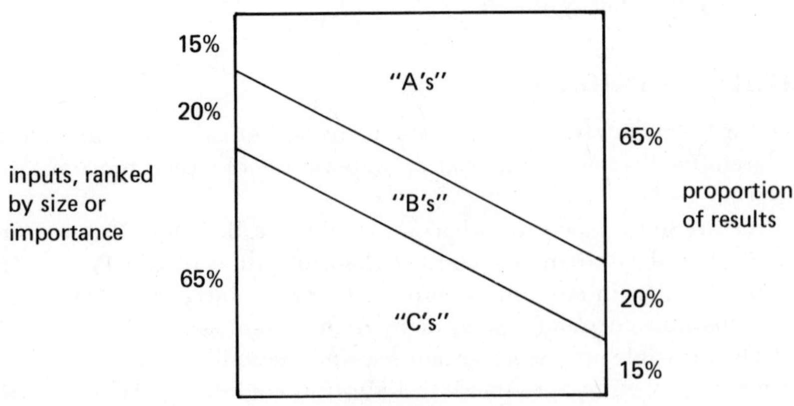

Figure 3-3
J. M. Juran's Principle of "the Important Few and the Unimportant Many"

Table 3-2
Functions Listed in Order of Importance

Function	*Classification*	*% of Time Now Being Spent on Each*	*Ideal Time To Be Spent on Each*

Table 3-3
Hypothetical Ranking of Typical Functions

Function	*Classi-fication*	*% of Time Now Being Spent on Each*	*Ideal Time To Be Spent on Each*
Planning	A		
Budgeting	A		
Making decisions	A		
Making sales calls	B		
Writing proposals	B		
Reading company reports	B		
Reading correspondence	B		
Writing reports	C		
Answering correspondence	C		
Telephone	C		
Training staff	C		
Salary administration	C		
Appraisal interviews	C		
Recruiting	C		
Purchasing	C		
Handling complaints	C		
Equipment	C		
Reading industry publications	C		
Community activities	C		

You will find that most of the "A" functions tend to be managerial in nature, such as analyzing, planning, and staffing; many of the "B" functions are supervisory in nature, such as observing, training, and correcting; most of the "C" functions are instances in which you personally are performing lower-level functions that could be delegated to the staff.

The next step is to calculate, from your time log, the percentage of time you spent in a typical week on each function. List the percentages in the appropriate column.

Now look at each function and ask yourself if you are spending too much, too little, or about the right amount of time on each function. If you are like most managers, you will identify some "A" functions you would like to spend more time on and some "B" and "C" functions that are taking up more time than their importance justifies.

After comparing the importance of a function with the time it has been consuming, decide how much time you would ideally like to devote to each function and enter that in the "Ideal Time" column.

An "A" function does not necessarily require three or four times as much time as a "C" function. Planning, for example, is one of the most important functions of a manager, yet planning may require only 5% of the manager's time. The important thing is not to let "C" functions crowd it out to such an extent that you are spending only 1% or 2% of your time on planning, or perhaps for long periods no time at all.

FIRST THINGS FIRST

Your objective now is to assign top priority to the "A" functions and get them done first, instead of getting so bogged down in the "C" functions that the "A's" are shortchanged.

There is a well-known story about an industrial engineer called Ivy Lee. Back around the turn of the century, he called on Charles M. Schwab, president of United States Steel Co., to offer his services in improving the efficiency of the steel company.

"I don't need anybody to tell me what needs to be done," Schwab replied. "I know exactly what I have to accomplish—my only problem is to find the time to do the things I know have to be done."

Lee said he had a suggestion that would help Schwab with his time problem. There would be no charge for the suggestion, Lee said, but if Schwab found it useful he could send Lee a check for whatever the idea had been worth.

A month later Lee received a check for $25,000 (the equivalent of perhaps $250,000 in today's dollars).

Here's the suggestion, free. First thing every morning, make a list of the *three most important things* you hope to accomplish during the day. Start working on the first one, and keep coming back to it after every interruption. When you finish the first one, start on the second one. But spend every available minute on those three priority tasks. If one or two of them are not completed, they go on the list for the next day.

Allen Lakein, noted time management consultant, calls this a "daily to-do" list and says it is habitually used by every successful executive.

This principle seems simple and even obvious, but it is important for this reason: There is a natural, human tendency to tackle the "C" functions first. They are easy, each one takes very little time, and often there is a certain urgency to them, so the manager says, "I'll get these little chores out of the way first so I can concentrate on the important ones later." At 5:00 many unimportant tasks have been completed, but the neglected "A" functions are tucked into the briefcase to be worked on in the evening—maybe.

HOW TO CUT DOWN ON "C" FUNCTION TIME

There are only ten ways in which you can handle a function or some part of a function in less of *your* time. Pick two or three of the "C" functions that are absorbing more time than you think they should. Write them down in the leftmost column of Table 3-4. Consider the first "time-eating" function. As you read through the following list of "Ways to Control Time-Eaters," ask yourself which of these methods might apply to *some part* of the time-eating function. Rarely will one of these methods apply to the entire function you listed, but usually two or three of them will apply to parts of the function.

Ten Ways to Control Time-Eaters

1. Eliminate

You can rarely eliminate an entire function, but often you can eliminate parts of one. Are you trying to keep up with four magazines in your field, when two or three would be enough? Do you belong to more business associations than are really necessary? Are you compiling some reports that are not worth the effort?

2. Delegate

A time trap into which many managers fall is spending time on minor chores that should be done by staff members. Always be looking for ways to systematize parts of your duties and turn them over to subordinates. And beware of "upward delegation," when staff members leave a task half completed, and naive managers finish it for them.

The principle of delegation is not limited to work you can assign to assistants. Look for parts of tasks that would be made easier if some piece of the activity was performed by customers, suppliers, or others outside the office.

3. Combine

Often two time-killing chores can be handled simultaneously. If you travel, you can do reading and paperwork while on the plane or train. The morning's mail can be scanned and sorted while making phone calls; there is usually some waiting time before you are connected to the person you want.

4. Bunch Similar Tasks

There are many minor tasks that take less total time if you wait until a number of them have accumulated. Let's say you receive occasional requests that involve obtaining data from files or reference books. Wait

Table 3-4
Controlling the Time-Eaters

	WAYS TO CONTROL TIME-EATERS										
Items Consuming Too Much Time	*Elim- inate*	*Dele- gate*	*Combine*	*Bunch*	*Handle as It Comes*	*Routin- ize*	*Find a Short- cut*	*Set a Time Limit*	*Estab- lish Prior- ities*	*Take It up with Your Boss*	*Plan for Follow-Through*

until you have a dozen similar requests, or save them all up until a regular time of the week. Then you can do all your assembling of facts at one time.

5. Do It Now

This is the diametric opposite of the "bunching" concept. Although some tasks take less time if you postpone and "batch" them, others take more time if postponed. When a minor decision needs to be made, for example, it is usually less time-consuming to make it immediately, when the facts are before you, than to postpone it and then have to search your memory or your files for needed information.

6. Routinize

If you find yourself doing similar tasks frequently, look for some routine way of handling them. If, for example, you find yourself writing or dictating a similar kind of letter several times a week, would a form letter serve the purpose?

7. Find a Shortcut

Is there some faster, simpler way of handling some task? For example, knowing that it costs $2 or $3 to prepare and mail a letter, wouldn't it often be faster and less expensive to reply by means of a station-to-station no-operator-assistance phone call?

8. Set a Time Limit

Many tasks lend themselves to this device. You decide that a particular function is worth X minutes and no more. Visits by sales representatives who call on you regularly might fall into this category; if you can get all the information you need, and be polite and considerate, within 10 minutes, terminate the call after 10 minutes. You might decide that a particular business magazine is worth only 10 minutes of your time; force yourself to scan it within that period.

9. Establish Priorities

Tackling the "A" functions first is really another means of reducing the time spent on the "C" chores. By the time we have done the important things, only limited time remains for the unimportant ones. We handle them more quickly, delegate them, or in many cases simply neglect them. Many of them should have been neglected anyway.

10. Take It Up with Your Boss

If the person to whom you report or the procedures of the company for which you work are consuming some of your time *unnecessarily,* make a constructive suggestion for handling the function in less time.

This is quite different from merely complaining about being overworked. It means coming up with a suggestion like, "If we make this revision in Form X, we can use a carbon of it to serve the purpose of Form Y, thereby completely eliminating Form Y and the time it takes."

You might want to use Table 3-4 to list a few specific tasks that are taking up too much of your time, then run across the column headings and put a check mark under each method that might apply to part of each task. It is not unusual to find that two or three of the "Ways to Control Time-Eaters" will apply to a single task.

MISCELLANEOUS USEFUL IDEAS

1. Do Not Confuse Urgency with Importance

Many of the "C" tasks have deadlines—get that letter in the mail by noon, make those travel reservations before 5:00, call Mr. Smith before lunch, and so on. But the "A" tasks usually do not have deadlines: reorganize the filing system, redraft the employment contract. This is one reason why "C" tasks are often tackled first instead of later. They are urgent, but relatively unimportant. Work on the important functions first, and use some of the ten control methods to handle the "C" tasks.

2. Do Not Take Your Briefcase Home at Night

This idea comes from the book *Getting Things Done,* by Edwin C. Bliss. Bliss points out that if you plan to take your briefcase home at night, this gives you a great excuse for postponing decisions after 4:00 P.M.—decisions that might be quickly handled if you knew you were not going to shove them into a briefcase.

3. Beware of the Trap of the Familiar or the Pleasant

A salesperson who is promoted to District Sales Manager tends to spend far too much time dealing with customers, because this is a familiar and comfortable task, and too little time on unfamiliar and unpleasant tasks like counseling sales personnel or revising the district marketing plan. Whenever you find yourself happily immersed in a task that is as comfortable as a pair of old shoes, ask yourself whether you are spending more time than you should just because the job is familiar.

4

Staff Utilization

Are your most talented people spending too much time on routine clerical duties?

Are your highest-paid staff members doing work that should be handled by lower-paid or part-time personnel?

Are some of your people inefficient because they are forced to switch back and forth among 15 or 20 different tasks?

If you plan to make a work simplification study of two or three office functions, which ones should you start with?

In short, do you really know where all the staff time is going?

There are two basic ways of reexamining the way you are using your staff:

1. You can make a checklist of the functions assigned to each staff member to make sure the work load is distributed in the most efficient manner, or
2. you can collect records on how much staff time is being consumed by each function and analyze the results.

MAKING A CHECKLIST OF ASSIGNMENTS

The first step in this method is to make a list of every function being handled in the office. In a large office you would make a separate study for each division or department. You might want to make a preliminary list and circulate it among the staff to see if they can suggest any time-consuming chores you have omitted.

Make yourself a chart like that shown in Figure 4-1, listing the functions in descending order of importance—from the most important at the top down to the least important at the bottom. Across the top of the page, list all the staff members, including yourself, in descending order of salaries, with the highest-paid person at the left and the lowest-paid at the right.

Figure 4-1 is a brief listing of office tasks to illustrate the method.

Function	*Owner*	*Assistant*	*Alice*	*Joe*	*Mary*	*Tom*
Planning	✓	✓				
Selling		✓		✓		
Hiring		✓				
Supervising staff		✓	✓			
Processing orders				✓		
Shipping				✓		
Accounts receivable					✓	
Accounts payable					✓	
Payroll					✓	
Bank deposits					✓	
Routine correspondence			✓			✓
Training new people		✓	✓			
Filing						✓
Maintaining office supplies						✓
Maintaining office equipment						✓
Answering phone/ receptionist					✓	
Running errands						✓
Making coffee						✓

Figure 4-1
A (Brief) Checklist of Staff Assignments

A more complete and useful list of tasks appears at the end of this chapter in Figure 4-4.

Now opposite each function put a check mark under the names of the individuals who perform that function. Then ask yourself these questions about the results:

1. Do the check marks tend to form a pattern running from the upper left of the chart (important people doing important tasks) to the lower right (less important people doing less important tasks)? Beware of marks at the lower left, indicating that highly paid people are doing unimportant tasks.

2. As you look horizontally along the row opposite each function, has the function been assigned to too many or too few people? Things that are "everybody's responsibility" often tend to be neglected.

3. As you look vertically down the column under each individual's name, are some individuals handling too many different tasks? Valuable minutes are lost whenever someone has to drop one task and turn to another one.

4. Is the work load fairly evenly divided?

5. Is each person spending as much time as possible on the activities in which he or she is especially competent?

This simple little checklist may reveal an unbalanced or inefficient assignment of jobs to people.

MAKING A TIME ANALYSIS

An actual analysis of the way in which time is being spent yields information of much greater value.

Be careful to explain to your staff exactly why you are doing this. It can be psychologically threatening to some people to realize that someone is analyzing the way they spend their time.

Make it clear that what you are doing is analyzing the distribution of functions among the staff and the manner in which functions are being performed, so that everybody's job can be made as interesting and pleasant as possible.

There are three ways of doing this: the diary method, the time log method, and the work-sampling method. Your objective in making the study will determine which is most practical for you.

The Diary Method

Each person is asked to jot down the starting and ending time of each task performed during the day. An example might look like this:

- 9:20–9:35 Answered inquiries for prices
- 9:35–9:45 Filed catalogs received in the mail
- 9:45–10:15 Took dictation from Mr. Smith
- 10:15–10:30 Coffee break
- 10:30–noon Typed Mr. Smith's letters

  . . . and so on.

Then you, or an assistant, can summarize the total time each person spends on each task. A master list of all tasks will help in the compilation.

The Log Method

Each person is given a sheet of paper like that shown in Figure 4-2 with columns divided into 15-minute or half-hour intervals. Column headings are determined by the nature of the office functions. Make it clear to your people that they are not expected to keep time to the minute; they are merely to record, for each 15-minute or half-hour period, what they were doing during *most* of that period.

Provide a code on the back of the form, based on your own list of duties, so that each employee need jot down only two or three letters to designate a task. Base it on your master list of tasks. Part of your code might look like this:

- MO = mail, opening
- MD = mail, distributing
- MA = mail, answering
- FC = filing correspondence
- FI = filing invoices
- FG = filing catalogs

A code actually used by a management consulting firm is shown in Figure 4-2.

In using either the diary or the log method, emphasize to the staff that they should update the record every hour or so. If they let it go for several hours, they cannot remember accurately what they were doing in the earlier intervals.

see codes on back

DAILY TIME RECORD

If space is needed for explanation, use asterisk and footnote at the right

Name ________________ Date ________

Production, Client and Job No.					Sales—Prospect Company	Promotion	Overhead	Comments or Explanations
Client								
Job #								
8:30-9:00								
9:00-9:30								
9:30-10:00								
10:00-10:30								
10:30-11:00								
11:00-11:30								
11:30-12:00								
12:00-12:30								
12:30-1:00								
1:00-1:30								
1:30-2:00								
2:00-2:30								
2:30-3:00								
3:00-3:30								
3:30-4:00								
4:00-4:30								
4:30-5:00								
5:00-5:30								
5:30-6:00								

PRODUCTION SUMMARY

Client	Job Desc. and No.	Code	Output	Total Hrs.	DO NOT WRITE BELOW

Figure 4-2
Time Log Code Used by a Consulting Firm

DAILY TIME RECORD CODES

WRITERS

CC – client conference
F – fact-gathering (reading client's material)
PL – planning
RES – research, in the field only
W – writing
E – editing
PR – proofreading
V – revising
SW – supervising writer
SA – supervising art
SPH – supervising photographer
PREC – planning recording
SPD – supervising production of physical materials
REC – recording

(Specify any others not listed)

ARTISTS

LD – layout/design
M – mechanicals
O – overheads
S – slides
ST – spec type
CD – comp dummies
SP – supervise production

(Specify any others not listed)

SALES

SR – sales research
PL – planning before a sales call
CL – sales call (in person)
PRO – proposal planning and writing

(Specify any others not listed)

PROMOTION

MA – mailing
BR – brochure
LU – luncheon (SEC or other business groups)
PU – publicity, article, public relations
SP – speech

(Specify any others not listed)

OVERHEAD

GEN – general
INT – interview
RDG – reading publications
TRNG – training new people
PL – planning meeting
VIS – visitor
CR – general correspondence, not for sales or a specific client

(Specify any others not listed)

Figure 4-2 (continued)
Code on Reverse of Form

With either method, after recording the time for a typical week, add up the actual number of minutes each person spent on each function.

The Work-Sampling Method

In this method, instead of having employees keep track of all their time, you take a sample of what they were doing at random intervals during the day. Suppose, for example, that 50 times during the week you—or somebody—note what Mary is doing. If on four of these times she is filing correspondence, it is reasonable to assume that 4/50ths of her time, or 8%, is spent filing correspondence.

Make up some forms like that shown in Figure 4-3. Down the left-hand side list all the tasks performed by the individual or group you are analyzing. You can use one of these sheets for each individual, or one for the entire group if all are performing similar tasks.

The time intervals must be randomly selected; if you took your samples on the hour and half-hour every time, you might get a skewed sample. Also, use different randomly selected intervals every day.

We have filled in some random time intervals on Figure 4-3, but in making up your own forms, just type "9: , 9: , 10: , 10: " across the top, leaving space after each hour to fill in your random minutes each day.

How do you write in minutes that are truly random? Simple. Eugene M. Kamy, an authority on office efficiency, suggests that you open a phone book at random and take the last two digits of successive numbers. For example, a sequence of ten numbers picked at random from the Manhattan phone book was:

685-8040
203-2191
738-6350
368-4407
283-2211
612-0591
920-4322
926-6305
674-4271
923-7124

Ignoring last two digits greater than 59, we get this series of random numbers: 40 50 07 11 22 05 24. So your work samples would be taken at 9:40, 9:50, 10:07, 10:11, 10:22, 11:05, 11:24, and so on. If two

	9:40	9:50	10:07	10:11	11:22	11:05	12:24	12:	1:	1:	2:	2:	3:	3:	4:	4:
Opening mail																
Distributing mail																
Answering mail																
Filing corres.																
Filing other																
Dictation																
Typing																
Conf.																
Phone, customer																
Phone, supplier																
Phone, other																
Personal																
Supplies																
Equipment																

Figure 4-3
Checkoff Sheet for Work-Sampling Study

Management

Establishing goals and objectives
Establishing policies and procedures
Making decisions
Supervising people reporting to you
Reporting to higher-ups
Staff meetings
Space planning; office layout

Personnel

Hiring
Training
Performance reviews; evaluation
Salary and benefits administration
Personnel records
Meeting government obligations (EEO, etc.)
Administering personnel policies

Clerical/Secretarial

Pick up, open, sort and distribute mail
Communications:
- Telex
- Facsimile
- Telephone
- TWX

Coffee making
Typing
Dictation
Maintaining inventory of office supplies/ordering
Receptionist/switchboard
Equipment maintenance
Collect and process outgoing mail (meter, etc.)
Process purchase orders
Data entry and processing
Travel arrangements
Daily follow-up; suspense file; tickler file

Marketing/Sales

Advertising
Mailings
Maintenance of literature, price lists
Customer service:
- Contact and follow-up
- Handling complaints
- Inquiry follow-up

Conventions and trade shows
Sales projections
Maintenance of client list and mailing list

Accounting/Finance

Budget
Accounts payable
Accounts receivable
Billing
Posting
Credit:
- Authorizing
- Managing follow-up

Bank deposits
Bank statements
Petty cash
Payroll
Tax returns
Financial reports
Plant and auto insurance
Collection
Posting to general ledger
Credit checks received
Deposit checks
Write checks
Approve checks

Orders

Order entry, mail orders, phone orders
Receiving and shipping
Order processing
Filing orders

Figure 4-4
List of Office Tasks

numbers happen to fall within one or two numbers of each other, substitute a different number for the second one; samples taken too close together may give you a duplicate reading of the same task.

Again, take readings for a week and total up the number of check marks opposite each task. Calculate what percentage of total marks each task represents; the equation, as you know, is

$$\frac{\text{no. of marks this task}}{\text{total no. of marks}} \times 100 = \text{percentage this task}$$

In analyzing the results, ask yourself the questions listed on page 30 for the "checklist" method. In addition, consider what functions are absorbing the greatest amounts of staff time. These are the logical subjects for a work simplification study.

5 Work Simplification

In most offices, many valuable minutes are lost each day because unnecessary, time-wasting steps have crept into routine procedures. By taking a careful "new look" at these operations, ways can often be found to simplify and speed up the procedures.

You may remember a book and a movie called *Cheaper by the Dozen.* They were about a pair of industrial engineers, Mr. and Mrs. Frank B. Gilbreth, and their 12 children. In those days, ferries and toll bridges often charged for each passenger in an auto. The Gilbreths requested, and usually got, a special fare by insisting that the tickets should be "cheaper by the dozen."

Around the turn of the century the Gilbreths developed a procedure for examining any routine operation and eliminating needless steps in it. The process is called "work simplification." Primarily, it consists of:

1. observing and flowcharting each step in the process,
2. analyzing the charts to identify unnecessary or time-consuming actions,
3. developing a simplified procedure, and
4. putting it into practice.

The process may seem a bit complicated as you read about it, but usually it takes you (or someone you delegate the job to!) only an hour or so to observe some repetitive process and make a flowchart of it.

Several managers of small offices, at the request of the authors, applied this procedure to four different office functions. They were able to develop better procedures that reduced the time per transaction by 25% to 40%. Can you spend an hour today on an analysis that may save half an hour a day for the next 12 months or so?

But before you start your analysis there is an important preliminary step.

GETTING STAFF ACCEPTANCE

People feel uncomfortable and even threatened when they feel they are being observed—particularly if the observer is taking notes. Before starting to analyze some routine office procedure, assure the staff that the analysis does not threaten anyone's job but will in fact make all of their jobs easier and more secure.

You might want to call a brief staff meeting to explain the following points:

1. Paperwork and processing take up a lot of valuable office time.
2. By making a careful analysis of some routine office procedure, it is often possible to work out simpler ways of doing it.
3. As a result, the work is easier, errors are less frequent, customers are better served, and everyone is better off.
4. Employees will make more money if they are on some kind of incentive program. Even if not, the size of their potential salary raises is certainly influenced by the profitability of the office.
5. Some office procedures will be studied, but the analysis will be directed toward the procedure itself, not toward the efficiency of the person performing it.

DETERMINING WHAT PROCEDURE TO ANALYZE

To demonstrate to yourself and your staff that the work simplification method really works, select some fairly simple process first.

Office functions that can be profitably analyzed by this method are those that:

- consume considerable time.
- represent a large volume of transactions.
- are repetitive in nature, so that it is possible to develop standardized methods of handling them.
- include a relatively high possibility of error.

If you hold a staff meeting to introduce the idea of work simplification, you might ask for suggestions as to which office procedures to analyze.

WHO SHOULD MAKE THE ANALYSIS?

It is important that the process be carefully observed, a number of times if necessary. The method will not work if you simply sit down and write a list of the steps in the process being studied. Reason: You will recall only the important, operational steps. You will not think of the unnecessary steps, the very ones you are trying to spot and eliminate.

Who should do this observing and analyzing? Perhaps the manager. Perhaps a senior staff member. Or, if several staff members perform the same function, perhaps they can observe one another.

OBSERVING AND CHARTING THE PROCESS

Make yourself a supply of duplicate copies of the form shown in Figure 5-1. Then, as you observe the process, write down *every single step* or action taken by the person handling the process. Enter the estimated or actual time taken by each step in the column provided, and the total time at the foot of the column. You may have to observe the process several times to make sure you have not overlooked anything.

Next identify each step as either an operation, a filing, an inspection, a transportation, or a delay. Gilbreth used symbols he called "threbligs" (Gilbreth spelled backwards—sort of). We have simplified his simplification by using the letters "O" for operation, "F" for filing, "I" for inspection, "T" for transportation, and "D" for delay. Here are the definitions of the five types of steps:

Operation: any step that moves the process nearer to completion; a necessary, productive part of the operation. In manually typing a letter, for example, inserting the stationery into the typewriter would be an operational step.

Filing: any step in which something is put into the files, taken out of the files, or consulted while remaining in the files or in a reference book.

Inspection: a step in which an operation previously performed is checked by that same person or another person.

Transportation: a step in which a person or object is moved from one place to another. For example, when a person walks to the office copying machine, that is a transportation step; running off a copy is an operation; walking back to the original desk is another transportation step.

WORK FLOW PROCESS CHART							Date Charted	Process Charted	Details of ☐ Present Method ☐ Proposed Method
Operation	Filing	Inspection	Transport	Delay	Time Required	Distance in Feet	YOUR COMPANY NAME HERE Department		
O	F	I	T	D					
O	F	I	T	D					
O	F	I	T	D					
O	F	I	T	D					
O	F	I	T	D					
O	F	I	T	D					
O	F	I	T	D					
O	F	I	T	D					
O	F	I	T	D					
O	F	I	T	D					
O	F	I	T	D					
O	F	I	T	D					
O	F	I	T	D					
O	F	I	T	D					
O	F	I	T	D					
O	F	I	T	D					
O	F	I	T	D					
O	F	I	T	D					
O	F	I	T	D					
TOTALS									

Figure 5-1
Work Flow Process Chart

Delay: a period of waiting time when nothing is happening, as when a document is lying in an out-basket, or typed letters are awaiting a signature.

Determine which of the five categories each step in the observed process falls into and circle or "X" the appropriate symbol for each step. Then connect all the circles or X's with a heavy zigzag line. Figure 5-2 is a hypothetical example.

Notice that the five symbols are arranged with the most productive steps at the left and the least productive ones at the right. Operation steps are the ones that get the job done; the higher the percentage of operation steps in the total process, the more efficiently it is being handled. Filing steps are usually necessary; inspection steps are less productive; transportation and delay steps are unproductive and often can be eliminated or reduced.

In short, the more closely the zigzag line that connects your X's adheres to the left-hand side, the more efficient the procedure; every time it touches the two right-hand columns, there is at least the suggestion that time is being wasted.

ANALYZING THE PROCESS

Now you examine each individual step in the process to see if it could be eliminated, shortened, or simplified. In making this analysis you use Rudyard Kipling's famous "serving men"—remember the poem?

I keep six honest serving men;
  They taught me all I knew.
Their names are What and Why and When
  And How and Where and Who.

We will use them in a different order, but essentially you look at *each step* in the process you have charted and ask yourself:

WHAT is being done here?

WHY is it being done? Could it be eliminated?

HOW is it being done? Why is it being done in this particular way? Is there a better way of doing it—a different method, a different form, a different kind of equipment?

WHEN is it being done? Would it be better to perform this step earlier or later in the procedure? Or to remove it from this process and handle it at some other time?

WORK FLOW PROCESS CHART							Date Charted 10/2/81	Process Charted Maintenance of Mailing List	Details of ☐ Present Method ☐ Proposed Method
Operation	Filing	Inspection	Transport	Delay	Time Required	Distance in Feet	YOUR COMPANY NAME HERE Department		
(O)	F	I	T	D			Pick up old client folders		
O	F	I	(T)	D			Transport folders to work area		
O	F	I	(T)	D			Pick up index & Scriptomatic files from cabinet		
O	F	I	(T)	D			Transport to typing area		
O	F	(I)	T	D			Check folders with 3x5 index cards		
(O)	F	I	T	D			If previous clients, enter trip data on index cards		
O	F	I	(T)	D			Take these folders to file		
(O)	F	I	T	D			Type Scriptomatic address masters		
O	F	I	(T)	D			Take masters to Scriptomatic machine		
(O)	F	I	T	D			Set up machine & make set of 3x5 cards		
(O)	F	I	T	D			Enter trip data on these 3x5 cards		
O	(F)	I	T	D			File new Scriptomatic masters by zip codes		
O	(F)	I	T	D			File 3x5 index cards alphabetically		
O	(F)	I	T	D			File new client folders in client folder file		
O	F	I	(T)	D			Return Scriptomatic & index card files		
O	F	I	T	D					
O	F	I	T	D					
O	F	I	T	D					
O	F	I	T	D					
TOTALS									

Figure 5-2
A Completed Work Flow Chart

WHERE	is each step being performed? Could it be handled faster somewhere else? Would steps be eliminated if people, furniture, or equipment were relocated?
WHO	performs this step? Should someone else be doing it instead?

DEVELOPING AND IMPLEMENTING THE NEW SYSTEM

After eliminating or simplifying steps, you can make up a new work flow chart of your revised procedure and estimate how many minutes you have saved. Use your "before" and "after" charts to explain the improved procedure to the staff. Get the staff together to compare the two methods and explain why the new one is better.

Help the staff put the new procedures into effect. Then follow up periodically to make sure the new procedures are being followed. People have a way of slipping back into old and inefficient habits or developing new and equally inefficient ones, so it pays to check up now and then.

6 Forms

Forms are a very efficient means of recording, transmitting, and retrieving information. Just imagine how much time would be lost if an individual memo had to be written each time a form was used! But forms tend to proliferate. Old forms, like old soldiers, don't die. They just clutter up files. In many companies, new forms are created in a jiffy, but old ones are harder to discontinue.

Not only is the number of forms a problem, but their design can cause difficulties. In an office handling hundreds of forms a day, a few seconds lost on each form as a result of faulty design can add up to a great many wasted minutes.

AUDIT YOUR FORMS

The first step is to collect one copy of every form used in your office—*every* form. You may be surprised at how many have accumulated over the years.

Now look at each form and ask yourself these questions:

1. Could this form be eliminated entirely? It is not unusual for a form to stay in use for months or years after the reason for its existence has disappeared.
2. Can this form be combined with another form? There are two versions of this possibility:

a. Two different forms are being used for a similar purpose. Suppose, for example, that there was one form for payment of an initial deposit and another form for payment of the balance. Obviously, one form, with a box where one could indicate whether the payment was a deposit or the balance, could serve both purposes.
b. Information is being copied from one form to a second form that serves a different purpose. Here a carbon of the first form might possibly replace the second form. The wording need not be the same on both forms. The original might be some kind of request; the carbon might be a follow-up reading "We have not yet received—." Material entered on the original would be applicable on the carbon. If some of the information on the original is confidential, it can be blocked out on some or all of the copies.

3. Do we need all the information requested on the form, or can some of the lines be eliminated?
4. If the form comes with carbon sets, do we need that many copies of the form—always? If a particular copy is needed only occasionally, it is currently cheaper to run it off on an office copier than to buy all the additional carbons only to discard most of them.
5. Can the design of this form be improved? This subject is covered fully later in this chapter.

BUY READY-MADE FORMS OR PRINT YOUR OWN?

Stationery supply stores offer a variety of printed forms such as telephone message pads, expense account forms, employment application blanks, and many others.

For simple forms like telephone memos, ready-made forms usually suffice. But for more complicated forms it is usually less expensive to print your own, particularly when you consider the amount of staff time that can be saved by using forms that are well designed to fit your specific needs.

Economical Sizes and Colors

As paper comes off the huge rolls in a paper mill, it is cut into "mill sheets," which are 34 by 44 inches. A printer usually buys paper in this size. Forms are not printed one copy at a time. The printer prints as many copies of the form as will fit onto a mill sheet and then cuts up the sheet into individual forms.

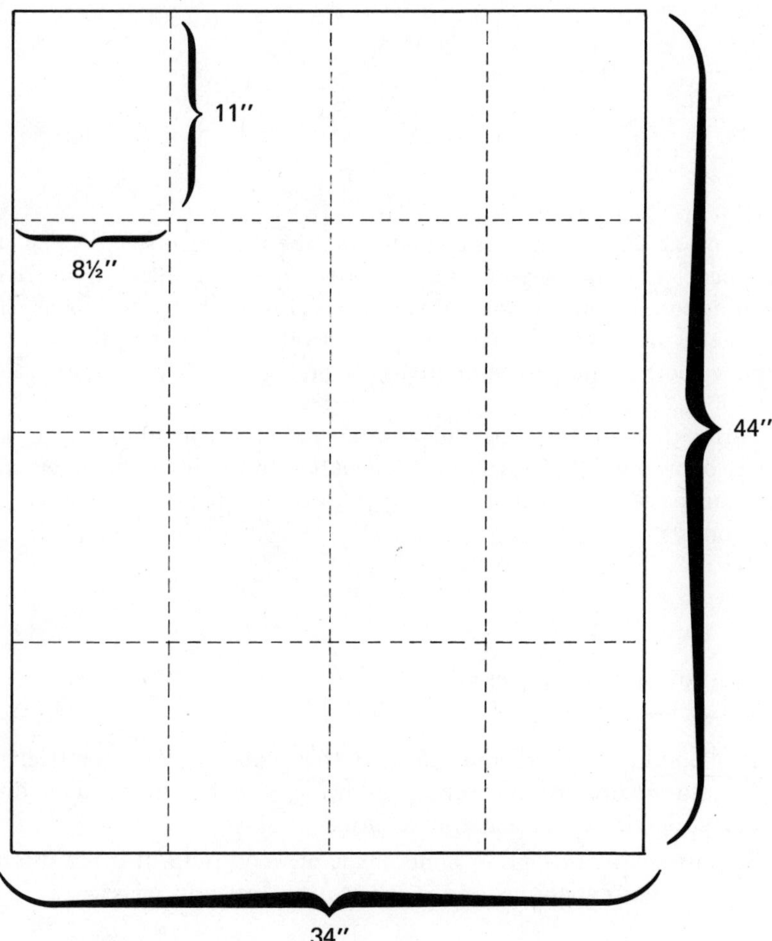

Figure 6-1
A Mill Sheet Divided into 8½ × 11″ Forms

For example, an 8½ × 11″ form will fit onto a 34 × 44″ mill sheet exactly 16 times (Figure 6-1). Instead of printing one form each time the press turns over, the printer prints 16 of these forms with every revolution of the press and then cuts the sheet into 8½ × 11″ forms. This reduces the cost per copy considerably.

Therefore it is less expensive if every form is some multiple or division of 8½″ × 11″. These sizes would be

- 11″ × 17″
- 8½″ × 11″
- 8½″ × 5½″
- 4¼″ × 5½″
- 4¼″ × 2¾″

If you design a form of some odd size, the printer first has to cut the mill sheet into the nearest multiple of 8½ × 11″, then do a second trimming operation to your freak size. This both wastes paper and increases printing costs. That is why practically all filing equipment and supplies come in multiples or divisions of 8½ × 11″ (except legal-sized sheets of 8½ × 14″).

Forms that are filed together should, of course, be of the same size. If it is occasionally necessary to file smaller forms in with larger ones, staple or paste the smaller form to a piece of paper the size of the larger ones.

Paper

The two basic types of paper are:

1. Rag bond, which contains 25% to 100% fiber or rags for strength. It is easier to erase on, resists yellowing, and has tremendous durability, but it carries a premium price.
2. Sulphite paper or register bond, made of wood pulp. It is less durable but also less expensive, and it is adequate for most office uses.

Other considerations in specifying paper: (a) grain, in paper made of wood fibers, which affects the stiffness of the paper; (b) opacity, which determines whether material on the reverse side, or the next page, will show through; and (c) reflectiveness, since entries on the form are more legible if the paper reflects light to the right extent.

How thick should the paper be? Paper thickness is described in terms of pounds per ream (480 sheets) of mill sheets; a 16-pound paper weighs 16 pounds per ream of mill sheets.

For a single-copy form, 16-pound weight is adequate. For multicopy forms or computer forms, the total weight of the paper and carbons should not exceed 90 pounds. For example, if the form has an original and four copies, and you plan to use typical 9-pound carbon paper, the four sheets of carbon would add up to 36 pounds. Subtracting 36 from the maximum of 90, you get 54 pounds, the maximum weight of the five pieces of paper. So you could specify 10-pound paper for each copy. Or, if you wanted the original copy to be heavier, you could use 16-pound paper for the original and 8-pound paper for the four copies: $16 + (4 \times 8) = 48$, which is well within the 54-pound limit.

Because of the continuing increases in postage costs, use the lightest possible paper to minimize mailing costs.

Colors of Paper and Ink

All printers carry a few colors of paper and ink as standards. If you specify a nonstandard color, it will cost you more. The color of the paper and ink should have the maximum contrast for best readability.

As to inks, most printers have a standard blue, red, and black. If you order a color that is not standard, the printer has to stop the press, clean it, insert the new ink, ink the press again, run your job, then clean up again before going on to a new job. You pay for all these operations.

Each printer also has four or five standard paper colors, such as white, blue, canary, sometimes goldenrod, and sometimes pink. By selecting one of your printer's standard colors, you avoid the extra costs of special handling.

The best contrast is achieved with black ink on white paper. We recommend it except when you want the copies to be of different colors to guide the distribution process.

DESIGNING THE FORMS

The Filing Key

The phrase "filing key" refers to the number or word by which the material is filed. This filing key should be located on the form in such a way that it can easily be located merely by thumbing through the corners of the cards or files, without having to remove them to locate the desired file.

As indicated in Figure 6-2, if the documents are in file folders or are bound in a loose-leaf book or a pasteboard, prong-type binder, the filing key should be at the upper right. This makes it possible to locate the document quickly by merely flipping through the tabs, without removing the file folder or opening the bound book.

For forms on index cards, kept in file boxes or merely wrapped with a rubber band, put the filing key across the top. To locate a desired card, you just flip through the tops or fan out the cards.

Hand-filled Forms

Allow for five letters or numbers per inch to allow space for clear, legible writing. Most people's names can be handled with 30 characters, so ideally provide a 6-inch line for names. Allow the same space for the address. Vertically, allow four lines per inch.

Forms Filled Out by Typewriter

Margins

Accounting machines, computers, and typewriters can take paper of a certain width, but within that width the type line itself is somewhat shorter, requiring a margin on both sides. For example, a computer may be able to take a form up to 18 inches wide, but the actual typing of data may be limited to 13.2 inches; so any form for that machine will require margins totaling 4.8 inches, or 2.4 inches on each side. Accounting machines and typewriters have similar limitations.

If you plan to bind the forms in a three-ring or similar binder, allow adequate space not only for the binding holes, but for the build-up of paper thickness on a prong-type binder that makes it difficult to open the pages out flat.

As a general rule of thumb, allow at least a 1-inch margin on the side that is going to be bound, a quarter of an inch on the opposite side, half an inch on top, and a quarter of an inch on the bottom.

Spacing

When there is inadequate space on a hand-filled form, you can do all sorts of things—print two lines in the space allowed for one, write in the margin, run an arrow to the top or bottom of the form and insert additional data there, and so on. But if you are filling out a form on a typewriter or accounting machine, the machine can print just so many characters in a horizontal inch and so many lines in a vertical inch. It cannot squeeze extra data into those limitations. So you must know in advance how much space will be required for each entry.

Horizontal spacing is determined by estimating the maximum number of characters that will be required for each entry. Most people's names, for example, can be handled with 30 characters. If your machine prints ten characters per inch, 3 inches will suffice for the "name" line.

If there is to be a space for "age," you know that not many people will be 100 years old, so space for two digits is sufficient. Similarly, 25 to 30 characters are adequate for most street addresses, because you can use abbreviations. Typewriters with pica-size type print ten characters per inch; elite type gets 12 characters per inch, but it is a good idea on forms to allow space for the larger pica characters.

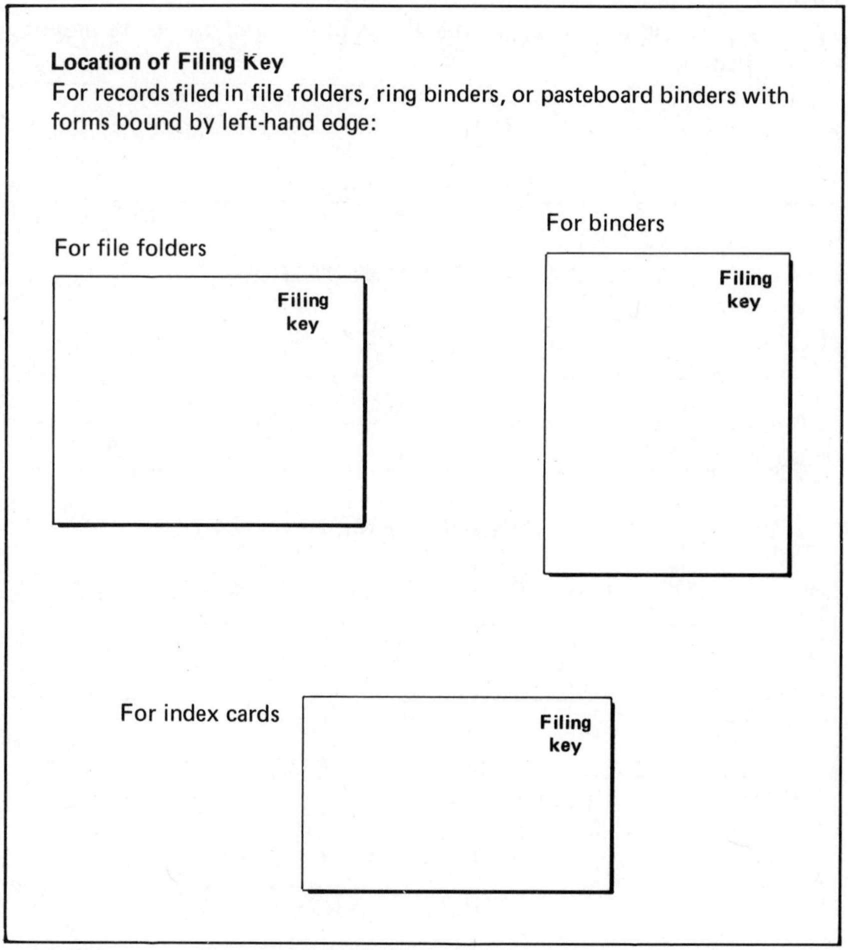

Location of Filing Key
For records filed in file folders, ring binders, or pasteboard binders with forms bound by left-hand edge:

For binders

For file folders

Filing key

Filing key

For index cards

Filing key

Figure 6-2
Location of Filing Keys

Vertical spacing, between the lines, should correspond to the vertical spacing on whatever machine will be used for the form. A typewriter prints six lines per inch; if you use this spacing on your forms, once the typewriter has been lined up for the first line, all the other lines will match up on the typewriter without the need for adjusting the roller.

If the form you are designing is to be filled out on a computer or bookkeeping machine, type a sample on your own machine to get the horizontal and vertical spacing. Bookkeeping machines may print 8, 10, or 12 characters per inch and six or eight lines per vertical inch.

Layout

What is the best way of arranging the captions and the corresponding space for entries?

Layout Style No. 1 in Figure 6-3 is the one most frequently used when people draw up their own forms. The caption appears at the left

DATA ARRANGEMENT METHODS

Your name ______________________________

Address ______________________________

Citizenship ______________________________

Layout Style No. 1

____

Your name

____

Address

____

Citizenship

Layout Style No. 2

Your name	**Address**
Citizen of U.S. ☐ Other (specify) ☐	

Layout Style No. 3

Figure 6-3
Types of Layouts

of the line on which the entry is to be written. This layout has two disadvantages:

1. The caption takes up too much of the space on the writing line, so that the entry may be cramped if in longhand or may incorporate too many abbreviations if machine printed.

2. The captions are of varying length. If the form is filled out by typewriter, each fill-in line starts some different distance from the left-hand margin, so tab stops cannot be used. The starting position of the typewriter has to be adjusted for each line; this wastes a lot of time.

In Layout Style No. 2, the caption appears below the line. Now all fill-ins start with the same left-hand margin, which makes that part of it easier for the typist. But the typist has to soft-roll the typewriter up one line to reach the caption, then return the roller to its original place to fill it in, or perhaps keep an extra blank copy of the form in view. In any case, productivity is reduced.

Layout Style No. 3, the so-called "box" design, is standard with most forms specialists. The caption appears in the upper left-hand corner of each box. As a result, the entire writing space is left open, and all lines have a common left-hand margin. If there are captions partway across the lines, arrange them with a common starting point so that the tab keys on the typewriter can be used.

By printing the caption in the upper left-hand corner of each entry, you avoid any confusion as to which space belongs with which caption, something that is not always clear with Layout Style No. 2. This third style is the most readable, time-saving format. Layout Style No. 3 also illustrates the use of the "ballot box" arrangement. Since most people you are dealing with will be citizens of the United States, you save time by merely putting a check mark in the box instead of writing out the country of citizenship. A second ballot box and fill-in line are provided for noncitizens. Be sure to locate the caption as near to the box as possible, so that the user knows where to enter the explanation.

Line Weight and Type Styles

Most of the horizontal lines on a form will be simple, single-weight lines, like those created by a ball-point pen or the underlining key of a typewriter. Bolder lines or double lines can be used to set off or emphasize parts of the information.

When a number of names or items are to be listed one below the other, make every fifth line heavier. Or, if there are no horizontal lines, insert a line after every fifth name. This makes it much easier for the eye to read horizontally across a row.

Sequencing of Data

This is important both with forms used wholly within your office and with forms that interact in some way with forms or data provided by someone else.

1. In copying data from somebody's Form 1 to your Form 2, arrange the data on your Form 2 in the same order and location as it appears on the outside Form 1. This will speed up copying the information.

2. Put all of the "always used" information at the left of the form; if there are some items that appear only sometimes, put them in the middle of the lines. This means that the typist can use the common left-hand margin for all the frequently used entries and has to skip out to the center of the line only when the less frequently used information must be entered.

PROVIDING COPIES OF FORMS

There are four ways of providing the necessary copies of forms:

Loose Forms

The typist can take the required number of loose forms, interleaf carbon paper, jog the forms and carbons into alignment, and insert them into the typewriter. Time is consumed in jogging the paper, inserting and aligning the set in the typewriter, then separating out the carbons and reinserting them in the next set. Anybody filling out many forms would probably be more productive by using one of the next three methods.

Padded Forms

If you print your own forms, ask your printer, instead of sending them to you loose, to put a piece of chipboard at the top of them, put some glue along the edges of the forms, and deliver them to you padded, in good registration (Figure 6-4). With these pads:

1. If forms are filled out by hand, you simply insert the number of carbons required and fill out the form without removing it from the pad.
2. If forms are typed, you remove the required number of copies, insert carbons, and type. The glued edge keeps the forms in alignment and eliminates jogging.

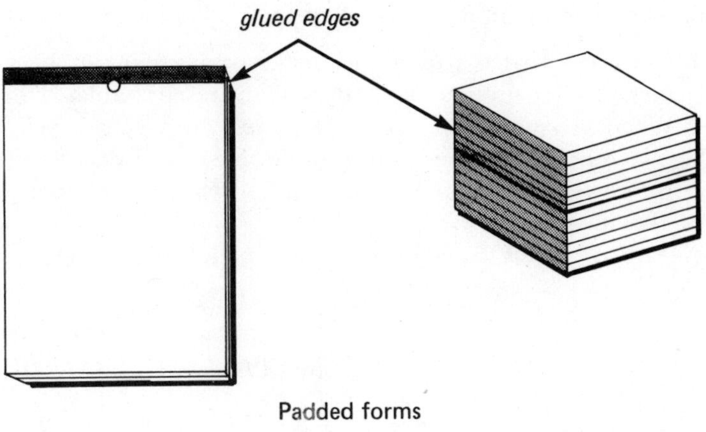

Padded forms

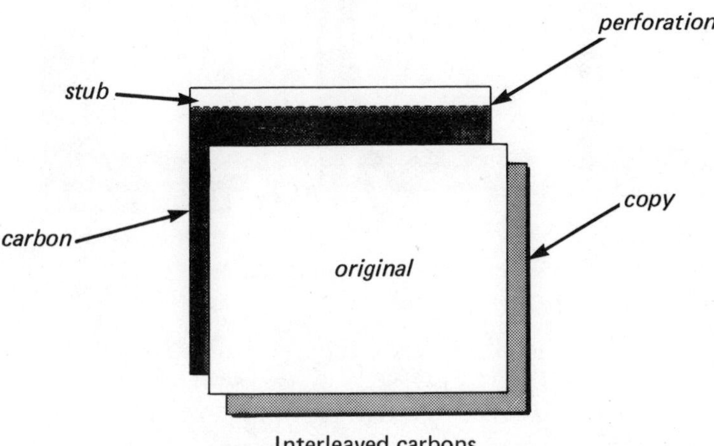

Interleaved carbons

Figure 6-4
Padded Forms and Interleaved Sheets

Interleaved Carbon Form Sets

Here the individual forms are interleaved with carbons and glued together to a stub, which holds carbons and forms in exact registration (Figure 6-4). You put the entire form set into the machine, type, and when finished, grab the stub and the bottom of the forms, pulling them apart. The carbons come out with the stub and are discarded; the forms are loose and ready for distribution. Although these sets save personnel time, they are expensive in terms of cost and inventory. The minimum order is usually 2,500 copies, so this method should be limited to forms that are repetitively typed in high volume.

Carbonless or "No-Carbon-Required" Papers

These are specially coated papers that make copies without the use of carbon paper. The coating contains dyes that are encapsulated in tiny capsules. When pressure is applied to the paper by a pencil, pen, typewriter key, or other hard object, the capsules break and deposit the dye on just the portion of the paper that has been written upon. This produces the image.

There are two basic types of carbonless paper (Figure 6-5).

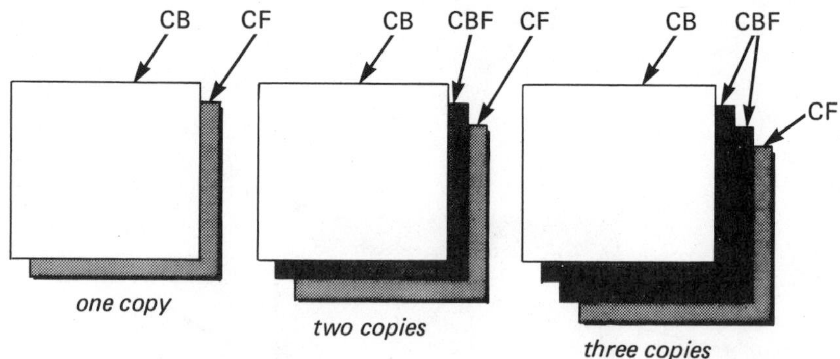

Two-Coated, or "NCR" Type of Carbonless Paper

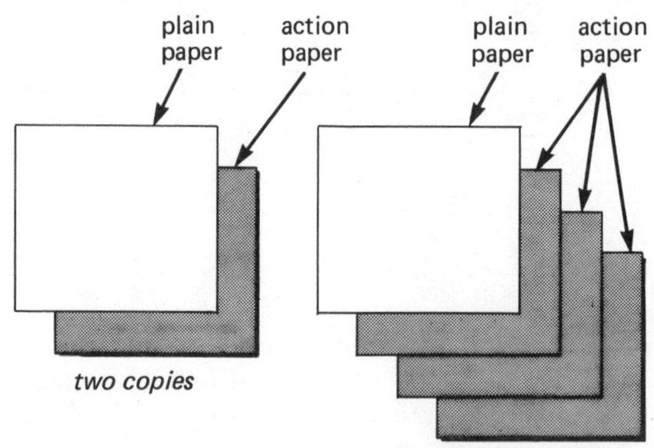

Action Paper or "3-M" Type of Carbonless Paper

Figure 6-5
Two Types of Carbonless Paper

The Two-Coated System

This is also called the "NCR" type. In this method there are two dyes, which must mingle to produce the image. One is coated on the back of one sheet, the other on the face of the sheet under it.

As shown in Figure 6-5, the first sheet—the one hit by the typewriter keys—is a "CB" or coated back paper. If only one copy is to be made, the second sheet is a "CF" or coated front paper. When a key is struck, the dyes from the back of the CB mingle with those on the front of the CF paper to produce the image on the CF paper.

If three or more copies are to be made, the papers between the first and last ones are coated on both sides and therefore are known as "CBF" paper—coated back and front. The front of each intermediate sheet receives one of the dyes from the sheet in front of it and transmits the other type of dye to the sheet behind it.

"Action" Paper or the "3-M" Type

Here the dyes are encapsulated separately, both dyes being coated on front of the second (or carbon) sheet.

Other Types

There are also the "blush-coated" and "physical transfer" types of carbonless paper. Table 6-1 summarizes the characteristics of the four types.

Any type of carbonless paper costs about 30% more than interleaved carbon-formed sets. For repetitive forms used in quantities of less than 2,500, carbonless paper can be economical if the cost is justified by the amount of staff time saved by eliminating the insertion of loose carbons into separate forms or padded sets. Virtually any printer can print carbonless forms for you; no special printing equipment is required.

Carbonless forms are extensively used where carbon disposal creates a problem. Banks, for example, have found that the use of carbonless papers for deposit and withdrawal forms eliminates the need for a guard to pick up discarded carbons.

Organizations that create classified records have minimized their waste disposal problems by using carbonless forms. With this practice they preclude the possibility that a readable carbon used to type classified information will be left in an unsecured location where it could lead to a security violation.

Data-processing installations have found carbonless forms valuable in those instances when an interleaved carbon form would be too bulky to be smoothly transported through either data-entry or forms-handling equipment. Conversion to a carbonless construction frequently reduces the form's bulk so that it can be processed in a single pass through the

Table 6-1
Types and Features of Carbonless Papers

Type	*Brand Names*	*Color of Image*	*Number of Copies Obtainable*			*Paper Weights Available*
			Handwritten	*Computer Impact Printer*	*Electric Typewriter*	
Blush-coated	Auto-Copy	Black	6	10	10	13-, 16-, 20-, 30-, and 48-pound
Physical Transfer	"ETC" Paper "IMPACT" Paper "CCC" Paper	Black or Blue	15	15	10	10-, 12-, and 14-pound
Two-Coated System	"NCR" Paper	Blue	6	6	10	15- to 26-pound
Self-Contained System	"Action" Paper	Black	4	6	10	10- and 12-pound bond

equipment. In addition, carbonless EDP forms reduce the forms-handling problems posed by carbon removal and disposal requirements.

In addition to their higher costs, carbonless forms have other disadvantages. They are limited as to the number of readable copies that can be made at a single writing. According to the process (pen, typewriter, etc.) used to create the image, this number will vary between 3 and 11 copies.

A problem with all carbonless forms is that you can create an image on a lower copy by accidentally applying pressure to the top sheet. If you have a pile of these sheets, for example, and are writing something on the top one with a ball-point pen, the image will be transmitted to a number of sheets. If the forms are padded, a piece of chipboard must be placed under the first one to prevent unwanted imaging on lower ones.

Erasures are difficult to make on carbonless forms; this precludes their use in applications where corrections are frequent. On this other hand, this difficulty of erasure is a safety feature, since any alteration in the copy is clearly evident.

ORDERING YOUR OWN FORMS

It is usually not economical to print your own forms on an office duplicator. Determine how many copies you should order at a time and then order padded forms, interleaved sets, or NCR paper.

Three Ways of Buying Your Forms

1. You can give a blanket purchase order to the printer running your forms. If you know how many copies of a particular form you will need throughout the year, you order that quantity but pay for them only as you withdraw them. The printer makes a saving on the large-quantity run and passes some of the saving along to you.

2. You can place individual orders for the forms as you need them. This is a somewhat more expensive purchasing procedure. According to the American Management Association, it costs about $40 to process a purchase order. This includes the costs of selecting the source, giving the order, verifying the invoice, issuing the check, and reconciling the check. Large-quantity orders obviously reduce the purchasing cost "per X thousand forms."

3. You can order ready-made forms from supply houses. Their catalogs include a great variety of forms; your company's name can be

printed on them. Of course, any unique forms requirement cannot be met by off-the-shelf forms, but ready-made forms can be used for some routine functions.

Economic Order Quantity

How many copies of a particular form should you order at one time? If you order small quantities frequently, you not only pay more per copy, but you also incur greater purchasing costs. If you order very large quantities, you tie up capital, use up storage space, and may have to discard some of the forms if they become obsolete.

If you get a price quotation from your printer for various quantities of a form or examine the prices for ready-made forms, you will find that the price per thousand drops rather rapidly as you go up from the minimum order quantity, but thereafter drops very little as the quantity is increased. It usually pays to buy only enough forms to get the major saving per unit, without worrying about the slight additional savings of the larger quantities.

If a clerk-typist is given authority to purchase forms, there is a tendency to order in quantities that are too large, just for the convenience of having an adequate supply on hand. The manager needs to explain carefully the unnecessary costs of overbuying.

7
Filing

Filing—putting documents into files and getting them out when they are needed—is an unavoidable function in most offices. It is an uninteresting task that should be delegated to the least expensive and least experienced members of your staff. Yet when something is misfiled and an important paper cannot be found, information retrieval suddenly becomes a Number 1 priority.

To help you reexamine and improve your own methods of information storage and retrieval, this chapter is organized as follows:

1. Some basic philosophies about filing
2. A checklist for evaluating your filing system
3. Basic filing methods
4. Filing equipment
5. Filing supplies
6. Records retention schedules for the United States and Canada

SOME BASIC PHILOSOPHIES ABOUT FILING

Categories of Files

In reviewing your overall filing system, place each type of document into one of these categories:

1. Active files, frequently referred to.
2. Inactive files, rarely referred to but occasionally needed to be accessible. Studies have shown that in most offices 98% of the references to a file take place within its first 2 years. After that it can be sent to some more remote (and less expensive) location.
3. Dead files, awaiting destruction in accordance with a records retention schedule.
4. Vital files that may be kept as long as the company is in existence—its corporate charter, real estate transactions, and so on.

The active files, and only the active files, should be handy to the people who use them.

Filing Is a Lower-Level Activity

If any appreciable amount of time is to be spent in filing materials and retrieving them, this work should be done by the lowest-paid employees. Of course, there will be instances when an executive or the executive's secretary will look in the files personally, but the routine filing of inactive materials should be done by those at the bottom of the pay scale, or even by part-time or temporary help.

Design Your Filing System with This in Mind

If the system is too complicated, the manager or the senior staff members may be able to use it effectively, but newer employees will need an executive's help in locating infrequently used documents. "If you can't quickly teach a high school student to do your filing on a part-time basis," one office manager comments, "then your system is too complicated."

Write the Filing Instructions

Many filing systems have simply evolved over the years, with something added here and something else removed there. The ground rules about what is to be filed, and where, exist mostly in the heads of the more experienced staffers.

One way to make sure your filing system is logical and complete is to write out a set of instructions that might be followed by a new employee. The process will not only clear the barnacles from the system, but the completed "standard filing procedures" will be useful in training new people.

What You File Is Your Business

You are under no obligation—to customers, to clients, to suppliers, or to employees—to file every piece of incoming third-class mail that has some relation to your work. File what you need and throw the rest away!

A CHECKLIST FOR EVALUATING YOUR FILING SYSTEM

How well does your filing system meet these seven basic criteria?

1. The filing system should be simple to install, operate, and use. The system should be so simple that it can be used by the newest or least intelligent person. It does not pay to develop a filing system so complex that the manager has to maintain it. The simplest method is always the best; the last thing you need is a filing system that requires a complicated manual of instruction.

2. The system should be adaptable to all types of records, regardless of their volume, frequency of use, or persons who file them.

3. The system should be capable of being revised easily. You must be able to add or delete topics or sections readily.

4. The system should be comprehensive. It must cover all the reference and communications needs of the office.

5. The system should be logically organized. It should enable you to bring subjects together that logically belong together.

6. The system should be effective and efficient in operation. You should be able to locate any individual record quickly and accurately—first the folder in which it is filed, then the document itself.

7. The system should be economical to operate. One of the worst things in the world is a system that costs more to install and more to maintain than the value of the information it feeds back to you. This is the big problem with some computer systems. The amount of money it costs to put them into effect can be greater than the amount you save by doing it.

There are two aspects of economy. First, there should be little, if any, need for costly auxiliary filing aids, such as an external card index to tell you where to find various files. Second, the filing system should make maximum use of standard office supplies and equipment. Specialized equipment often is costly to maintain.

BASIC FILING METHODS

A filing system is simply a continuing method of classifying, coding (marking), and filing records. It is designed to enable you to file and find papers. If you take your incoming mail and sort it by major functions—payments, receivables, client correspondence, etc.—you have taken a mountain of paper and reduced it to several smaller hills of paper. The idea behind any filing system is exactly the same: to sort the documents into small enough quantities that you can quickly locate the desired document within any category.

There are five methods of filing, and your office may well use all five of them for different kinds of files. We will first describe the five basic systems, then consider when a typical office might use each one.

The two basic methods of filing are alphabetical and numeric. Within each file there can be subclasses, which again can be either alphabetical or numeric.

In designing a filing system "from scratch," you go through these steps:

1. Decide whether to use alphabetical or numeric filing.
2. Decide which subclassifications you will use.
3. Decide what type of guide or folder arrangement you wish to use.
4. Select the appropriate filing equipment to implement your design.

The five systems are explained next.

Alphabetical Filing

Here everything is filed by the name of the person, firm, or whatever. In a customer file, the tabs run "James, Jones, Josephson." You create the subject heading at random and file it alphabetically. No attempt is made to correlate one topic with any other topic. If a geographical file were kept in strict alphabetical order, for example, "Samarkand," "Samoa" and "Samos" would be together.

The alphabetical system, while simple, has its limitations. It should generally not be used if the total file occupies more than one drawer. If it does, it fails to bring related data together and thus requires a lot of cross-indexing or searching.

An exception to this general rule is the case in which all the information filed alphabetically is similar in nature. It would be practical, for example, to have three or four file drawers full of information on the various states of the United States, filed alphabetically by state.

Numeric Filing

In this system the records are filed by number, using some serial number that has been preprinted on the document itself. This method is suited to financial records: purchase orders, invoices, cancelled checks. Numeric files should be limited to this type of document. People who were in the Army during World War II became accustomed to numeric filing and sometimes try to adapt it to correspondence files: you give each customer a number and retrieve his or her file by looking up that number. The trouble here is that you still need an alphabetical index of customers to give you their filing numbers.

Geographic Filing

This is a variation of alphabetical filing in which, for example, you might file catalogs or correspondence by country. Everything pertaining to a country goes into that country's folder, and the folders are filed alphabetically.

To prevent this system from becoming too cumbersome, countries can be divided into major zones of the world: North and South America, West Indies, Europe, Asia, Africa, Australia/New Zealand, and Oceana, for example.

Date or Chronological Files

This is really a variation of numeric filing. Documents are filed by date as a "tickler file." Its principle uses are for follow-ups and for keeping track of a sequence of steps in a prolonged process.

When May 26 arrives, for example, the tickler file for May 26 may remind you to get in touch with a major supplier about renewing a contract, to remind the maintenance service that office machines are due for servicing, and so on.

Subject Filing

This is another version of the alphabetical file, in which documents are classified in terms of the general subject they relate to. It lends itself to administrative records on payroll, taxes, invoices, and the like. There are two versions of the subject file:

1. Straight alphabetical. Each folder has a title such as "Payroll Records," "Tax Records," etc., and these are filed alphabetically. The difficulty with this system is that you are never sure that two people—or the same person at different times—will give the same classification to a document. If you have requested bids on intercom equipment, for example, you might start an "Intercom" file. When you are away and some correspondence on that subject arrives, your secretary may decide to file it under "Office Equipment" or "Contracts." If the number of subject titles is unrestricted, it is easy to create such multiple classifications.

2. Functional subject classification. In this system, all administrative records are subdivided into five or six basic functions, and *everything* related to one function goes into the file. The functional subjects would be broad classifications such as "Personnel," "Marketing," or "Accounting and Finance." The main advantage of the functional file is that it brings together in one filing location, one file behind another, all records related to the same functional subject.

The functional filing system lends itself well to reference materials such as business records, memos, and reports. If this material is filed alphabetically, the files tend to become unwieldy. One labor union filed documents under 2,500 classifications, necessitating the maintenance of a large card index file.

The strict alphabetical method can sometimes be ambiguous. Are records about the New York City sales tax filed under "T" for "Tax," "S" for "Sales Tax," "C" for "City Sales Tax" or "N" for "New York City Tax"? In a functional system, all tax information would be filed in the same place.

The authors have found that virtually any organization's records can be logically assigned to one of these 18 primary classifications:

- Accounting
- Administrative Services
- Associations
- Corporate Administration
- Data Processing
- Facilities, Properties, and Real Estate
- Financial Planning
- Government Relations and Legislative Matters
- Legal
- Operations

- Personnel and Industrial Relations
- Procurement
- Production and Manufacturing
- Public Relations and Community Affairs
- Research and Development
- Sales and Marketing
- Status and Control Reports
- Traffic and Distribution

These are subdivided into secondary topics, as required. For example, "Personnel" might be broken down into:

- Compensation
- Employee Benefits
- Employee Records
- Employment
- Environmental Health and Safety
- Industrial Relations
- Job Descriptions
- Organization Charts
- Training and Development

FILING EQUIPMENT

There are two basic types of files (Figure 7-1):

1. The standard drawer file, in which letters, forms, and other documents are placed in manila file folders and dropped into the drawer. To retrieve a document, you locate the appropriate manila folder by means of its title on a projecting tab and lift the desired document out of the manila folder. Usually, it is not necessary to lift the folder out of the file to remove one document from it.

2. The lateral file, in which the drawer pulls out from the "side" of the file. The drawer contains file folders suspended from metal hangers that slide along a bar. Two or three manila folders can be inserted into each of the hanging files. The primary advantage of the lateral file is that it occupies less space. The standard drawer file is 28 inches deep, but another 28 inches must be allowed in front of the file so that the drawer can be pulled out fully for access to the docu-

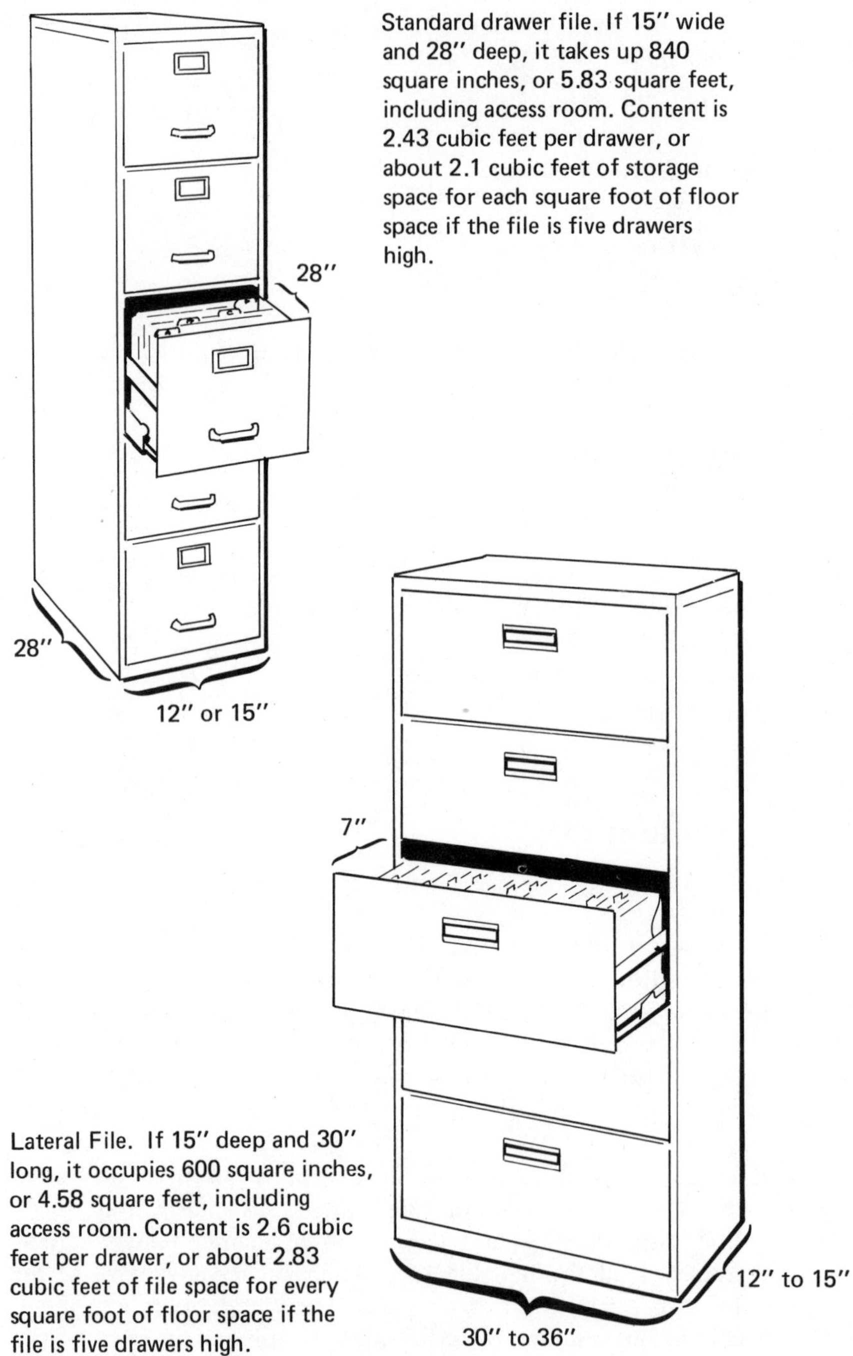

Standard drawer file. If 15″ wide and 28″ deep, it takes up 840 square inches, or 5.83 square feet, including access room. Content is 2.43 cubic feet per drawer, or about 2.1 cubic feet of storage space for each square foot of floor space if the file is five drawers high.
28″
28″
12″ or 15″
7″
Lateral File. If 15″ deep and 30″ long, it occupies 600 square inches, or 4.58 square feet, including access room. Content is 2.6 cubic feet per drawer, or about 2.83 cubic feet of file space for every square foot of floor space if the file is five drawers high.
12″ to 15″
30″ to 36″

Figure 7-1
Comparison of Standard and Lateral Files

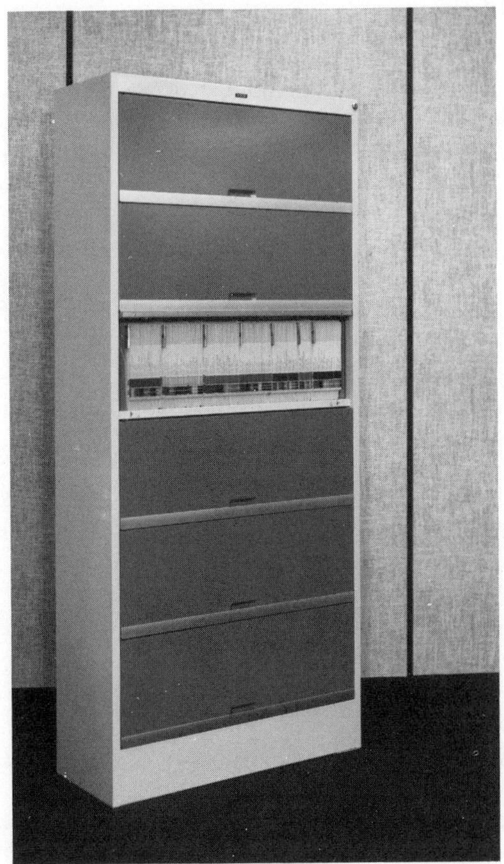

Figure 7-2
Lateral Files *(Courtesy Oxford Pendaflex Corporation)*

ments in the rear. The lateral file is only 12 to 15 inches deep, and the drawer pulls out only 16½ inches. The lateral file takes up 33% less space but provides 40% more filing area. The equipment costs more; but on the basis of equipment cost per cubic foot of filing space, it is actually less expensive.

Because the drawers of lateral files extend only 7 inches, these files can be placed along aisles or corridors, and employees can retrieve documents from them without blocking traffic. The files can also be used as space dividers. The lateral file lends itself to an attractive office layout. It looks more like a piece of office furniture than like a file cabinet, especially if plants or bookcases are placed on top.

FILING SUPPLIES

The principal supply item for both types of files is the standard manila folder with a tab at the top on which to write the contents of the file. With the lateral file you also need the Oxford-Pendaflex cardboard hanger that holds the manila file folders. These hangers are bulky—they take up about one-fourth of the space in each drawer—but the system overall provides better accessibility and saves floor space.

Since the hanging file folder costs about 40¢, it is usually reused. A manila file folder costs about 5¢; when its contents are no longer needed, the folder can be discarded; or it can be reused by pasting a gummed label for a new title on the tab.

In purchasing file folders you want folders that will be sturdy enough for the job, but not unnecessarily expensive. Since most of your records are of a transitory or temporary nature, you can follow these rules of thumb:

1. For documents to be retained 2 to 6 years, use a kraft (the dark brown kind) file folder of 11-point weight with a one-third center-cut tab. It is sturdy enough and less expensive than the white or tinted manila folders.
2. For records that will be kept less than 2 years, use a 9½ point manila folder with a one-third center-cut tab. It is suitable for temporary records that will not be referred to very frequently.
3. For records that will be used frequently or will be kept more than 6 years, there are two alternatives:
   a. For normal usage, select an 18-point kraft file with a center-cut tab. It is almost twice as heavy as the 11-point kraft and will last indefinitely under ordinary usage.
   b. If the file is used continuously, use a 25-point pressboard file. This is ordinarily blue; it has a metal tab on top and is virtually indestructible.

To subdivide a file drawer into major portions, use *file guides.* These are pieces of heavy (25-pound) pasteboard with a tab that projects up. The tabs are labeled to divide a whole file drawer into sections that might contain ten or twelve folders each. Make extensive use of file guides. Studies have shown that they save enough time to repay their cost within 3 months.

DEAD FILES AND RECORDS RETENTION

Governmental agencies require the office to keep various records for periods of time ranging from 1 year to almost perpetuity (in the case of real estate transactions, for example).

Dead Storage

Since these retention periods are usually much longer than the time during which the office actually uses the records, they should be placed in dead storage when no longer needed for day-to-day reference.

For easy storage filing, there is available a small carton known as the "cubic foot carton." It costs about $1.50 and has tremendous strength and durability. Such cartons are ideal for dead storage in some out-of-the-way place.

Records Retention Schedules

Most companies keep documents in their files longer than necessary—and what you keep that should have been destroyed can hurt you!

The Internal Revenue Service, for example, requires that records on income, deductions, and credits be kept for 3 years after the date on which the tax was due. For example, the 1980 tax was due on April 15, 1981. After April 15, 1984, those 1980 records can be destroyed, although most firms keep them for 6 years, which is the statute of limitations in most states. Whatever period you decide upon, make sure files are destroyed at the end of that time.

If you are audited, you are within your rights if you have destroyed files more than 3 years old. But if you have kept them, the IRS can use any information they find in your old files. When a brokerage firm was audited some years ago, auditors discovered tax records dating back 30 years—and the company had to pay $750,000 in back taxes based on information that should have been destroyed.

Many managers think "we have to keep everything 7 years" or "until the statute of limitations expires." That is not true. Required retention time varies from 1 year in the case of time cards up to "forever" in the case of real estate titles.

Each year the U.S. General Service Administration publishes a special edition of the Federal Register called "Guide to Record Retention Requirements." It can be obtained for $4.75 from the U.S. Government Printing Office, Superintendent of Documents, Washington, D.C. 20402. The 126-page 8½ × 11″ paperback volume has an index at the back ranging from "Accidents, Aircraft" to "Zuni Indians." Look up any subject in which you are interested, and you will be referred to a brief paragraph elsewhere in the book telling how long records on that subject must be retained and citing the federal regulation establishing that retention period. The federal regulations usually exceed the requirements of the states, or your own business requirements, so you are safe if you observe them.

"The period that (I.R.S.) records should be kept varies from a few years to a length of time that may cover more than one taxpayer's life-

Table 7-1
Typical Record Retention Schedule

(Copyright © 1975, 1976, 1977, 1979, and 1981 by the American Institute of Certified Public Accountants, Inc.)

Description	*Retention Period in Years*
Accounting records	
General ledger	Permanent
Clients' invoices	7
Payroll journals and ledgers	Permanent
Data transmittal (in central processing system)	7
Expense report	7
Time report	7
Other charges to clients' voucher	7
Accounts receivable adjustments voucher	7
Bill draft	7
Voucher check copies	7
Journal voucher	Permanent
Interoffice client charges	7
Client coding form—masters	1 + current
Payroll data and authorization	7
Correspondence	1 + current
Cash receipts and disbursements journals	Permanent
Billed accounts receivable aged trial balance	7
Client unbilled receivables ledger	7
Unbilled accounts receivable status	7
Employee time analysis	7
Analysis of billing adjustments	7
Client charges and billing report	7
Analysis of gross and net fees by service classification	7
Annual financial reports	
Partnership tax returns, annual statements and work papers—operating offices and consolidated	Permanent
Monthly or periodic financial reports	
Monthly statements—operating offices	7
Interim statements—consolidated	7
Other periodic financial reports	3
Supplemental accounting data	
Daily cash reports, remittance advices and bank deposit slips	1
Vendors' invoices, cancelled checks and petty cash slips	7[a]
Current legal documents	
Partnership agreements	Permanent
Leases and insurance policies	Permanent
Special contracts	Permanent
Noncurrent legal documents	
Partnership agreements—superseded	Permanent
Leases and insurance policies—expired	7[b]

Table 7-1 (continued)

Description	*Retention Period in Years*
Personnel data	
Personnel data, applications and contracts	
Present employees	Permanent
Personnel data—former employees	7
Employment applications—rejected	1
Miscellaneous	
Partnership meetings files (annual and special meetings)	7
Daily mail and attendance records	1
New business reports	Permanent[c]
Interoffice correspondence	Permanent[c]
Bulletins to clients, partners and staff	Permanent[c]

[a] Ordinarily, cancelled checks and paid vendors' invoices are destroyed after seven years. However, checks and invoices for purchase of assets, where the determination of basis might be important in the future, are retained indefinitely.
[b] The retention period for expired leases and insurance policies has been arbitrarily established to coordinate with other items. It should be noted that these retention periods are merely recommendations. Retention is necessary only until there is reasonable assurance that no further claims or disputes exist under the particular contract.
[c] Retain only one copy permanently—destroy balance.

time," the booklet explains. "The general requirement . . . is that records must be kept 'so long as the contents thereof may become material in the administration of any internal revenue law.' Some books and records of a business may be 'material' for tax purposes so long as the business remains in existence. . . .

"Records of property for which a basis must be determined to compute gain or loss upon disposition (and depreciation, amortization or depletion allowed or allowable) must be retained until a taxable disposition is made. . . .

"Records of income, deductions and credits (including gains and losses) appearing on a return should be kept, at a minimum, until the statute of limitations for the return expires. 26 CFR 301.6501(a)-1 provides the general rule that the amount of any tax imposed by the Internal Revenue Code shall be assessed within three years after the return was filed. . . .

"However, there are many exceptions. For example, a 6-year period of limitation applies for assessment if there has been a substantial omission of income . . . and a 7-year period applies for filing a claim for credit or refund relating to bad debts or losses on securities."

There are other retention requirements, mostly for shorter periods. In the United States, for example, if you advertise to fill a job, the antidiscrimination laws require you to keep copies of the ad for 1 year. If you give job specifications to an employment agency, data on applicants must be kept for 3 years. The IRS can ask a company to extend the retention period voluntarily on a specified return; such a request is usually granted.

A suggested records retention schedule for typical documents is given in Table 7-1; check it with your attorney. It is included by courtesy of the American Institute of Certified Public Accountants, Inc.

The important point is to have a written records retention policy and enforce it. Make a list of every type of document filed, and opposite each one indicate how long it should be kept.

As documents are put into dead storage, segregate them by the destruction date. One file or storage carton, for example, will contain all documents to be destroyed after April 15, 1984; another those to be destroyed in 1985; and so on.

8

Correspondence

The handling if incoming and outgoing mail is a function that absorbs a great deal of time in most offices. It can often be made more efficient by taking that "new look" at habitual procedures.

INCOMING MAIL

Managers of small offices sometimes insist upon opening and sorting the mail themselves. "It keeps me posted on what's going on," they will tell you.

This is an example of using the highest-priced personnel to do the lowest-skilled function. If it takes the manager 15 minutes a day, and if the total time cost including overhead is 50¢ a minute, it is costing the office 15 × 0.50 × 225 working days in a year (usually) for a total of $1,687 per year for the manager to perform this menial task. If the office is selling some product or service and netting 10% on sales, this loss is equivalent to the profit on a $16,870 sale.

A low-paid employee, even a part-timer, can open and distribute the mail if written guidelines are provided. If some letters may be confidential, the guidelines can specify that first-class mail (only) is to be left for the manager to open.

A typical set of guidelines might cover the following:

First-Class Mail

Route to the manager, unopened, or open it and distribute as follows:

1. Letters containing checks: staple the letter, check, and envelope and forward to the bookkeeper.
2. Letters addressed to individual staff members: do not open if marked "Personal"; otherwise open and forward to the staff member, or forward to the manager for a preview if that is what the guidelines specify.
3. Inquiries re prices, orders, etc. Forward to the Order Department.

Brochures Received in Quantity

1. If new, circulate one information copy to appropriate personnel; file the rest.
2. If a new supply of an existing brochure, file.
3. Discard the following types (specify).

Catalogs and Price Lists

File as specified.

Periodicals

Specify circulation and filing of each.

Mail Slitters

If the volume of mail justifies it, you can purchase or lease a hand-fed envelope slitter or mail opener. Slitters with an automatic feed are required only where there is a very large volume of mail to open.

Without a mail-opening device, the person who is manually opening the mail inserts a letter opener into one corner of the envelope, slits it open (sometimes slitting a letter or check in half), blows the envelope open, removes or shakes out the contents, and looks into the envelope again to make sure nothing has been missed. The electric mail slitter accomplishes all this in much less time.

Estimate how many minutes a day it takes the person handling the mail to slit the envelopes, multiply this by that person's cost per minute, multiply by 225 days a year, and compare that cost with the cost of owning or leasing a letter slitter.

Scheduling

If mail is delivered or picked up at the start of office hours, employees in some offices waste most of the first half-hour of each day waiting for their mail. The obvious, but sometimes overlooked, time-saver here is to have the mail-opening and distributing person come in an hour earlier than the rest of the staff and leave an hour earlier.

Attaching the Envelopes

Envelopes containing third-class mail are usually discarded, but it is often a good idea to staple the empty envelope to the contents of all first-class letters—certainly to those containing checks, vouchers, or orders. The envelope may carry a postmark, a notation, or even a return address that may be needed by the person handling the correspondence.

Individuals mailing a check with a letter or order form may neglect to fold the check into the letter. It is then possible to remove the letter and leave the check in the envelope. Even if this is double-checked, stapling the envelope to the letter eliminates the possibility of accidentally discarding something of value.

Presorting

Usually, the contents of incoming mail must be distributed among several locations—different offices, people, or file cabinets. Many steps can be eliminated, and many minutes saved, if the mail is presorted into bins or holders that can then be carried to the appropriate office or file drawer.

A simple presorting device, which takes up only about 1½ feet of desk space, is shown in Figure 8-1. It consists of six or eight plastic trays

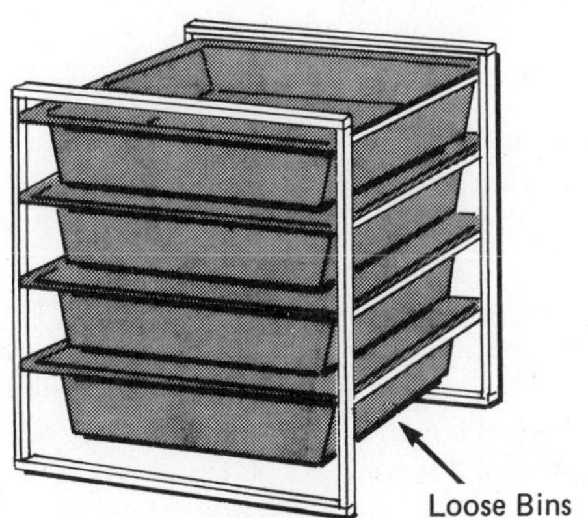

Figure 8-1
A Homemade Presorting Bin

(if nothing else is available, buy small plastic dishpans) that sit loosely on shelves. After the mail has been presorted into these trays, each tray can be carried to the file or office that receives that type of material.

The "FYI" File

Incoming mail often contains announcements or brochures with which everyone in the office or department should be familiar. This material must be circulated "FYI"—for your information. There are several ways of circulating one sample copy of this material; make sure you are using the method that is most efficient for your size and type of office. The methods are as follows.

1. Use the "buck slip" method. A buck slip is a rubber-stamped or printed form that gives the initials of each person who should see the document, with a space after each initial so that the person can put a check mark after his or her name before passing it along to the next individual. Preprinted buck slips can be stapled to the documents, or the form can be rubber-stamped onto the document. The documents pass from desk to desk, accumulating on the desks of persons who are out of the office.

2. Post a copy of the announcement on the office bulletin board. The copy may have a buck slip on it, to be initialed by each staffer as he or she reads the message.

3. Put each day's FYI notices in a glassine envelope, or a small tray or bin, and circulate it from desk to desk.

OUTGOING MAIL

Efficiency in handling outgoing correspondence simply means that every written communication is handled in the least expensive way possible, subject to such considerations as customer goodwill and the "image" the office wishes to create.

An individually hand-typed letter is the most expensive form of outgoing mail. When you add up the time involved in dictating the letter, typing it, proofreading it, often correcting or changing it, retyping it, mailing it, and filing the carbon, you will find, according to various estimates, that the individual letter costs $4 or $5.

How can you use less expensive substitutes for hand-typed letters? Word-processing equipment is one answer, as covered in a later chapter, but are there are any other shortcuts you might be using more frequently?

The first step, as is usually the case in seeking more efficient practices, is to "take a new look"—in this case keep a log of all outgoing correspondence for a week or two. Classify letters as to the functions they perform: answers to inquiries, price quotations, requests for information, covering letters for printed documents, and so on.

Substitutes for Hand-Typed Letters

Listed below are eight substitutes for hand-typed letters. Consider each of the items on your log of outgoing mail, and ask which of these substitutes might be used instead of letters:

1. Speedletters

Many businesses make frequent use of "speedletters" (Figure 8-2). A speedletter is a three-part carbon snap-out form with space for a question or other message at the left and for the answer at the right (sometimes question at the top, answer at the bottom). The person originating an inquiry puts the question on the left-hand side, keeps one carbon, and sends the original and one carbon to the recipient. The recipient writes or types the answer on the right-hand side, returns one copy to the originator, and files or discards the extra copy.

This is convenient to both the sender and the receiver, because the question and answer appear side by side on one short piece of paper.

2. Returning the Original

When an incoming letter asks for information, consider merely jotting the answer at the bottom of the letter and returning it to the sender. If a copy is needed for your files, run one off before returning the letter.

Like the speedletter, this practice has the advantage of keeping the question and answer on the same sheet. When the answer is embodied in a separate letter, the inquirer sometimes has to refer to a carbon of the original letter to determine exactly what was asked.

3. Printed Form Letters

Many routine inquiries, whether incoming or outgoing, can be handled by means of preprinted form letters. If they are printed on attractive letterhead paper with some thought as to the design, they can appear inviting and friendly rather than cold and mechanical.

Blank spaces can be left in the form letter for inserting specific information as to dates, prices, and such, which vary from letter to letter. A number of business printing firms offer a wide variety of printed form letters.

NCR - NO CARBON REQUIRED

FOR #10 WINDOW ENVELOPE MAILING, FOLD AS INDICATED IN BLUE PANEL BELOW

| ← IF USING TYPEWRITER, SET TAB STOP AS INDICATED

SHORT-KUT NOTE

☐ REPLY IMMEDIATELY

☐ REPLY BY ____________

☐ REPLY NOT NECESSARY

ALVIN MYLES JONES
CERTIFIED PUBLIC ACCOUNTANT
965 WALT WHITMAN ROAD
MELVILLE, N. Y. 11747

TELEPHONE 421-1200

TO

DATE: ____________

ATTENTION: ____________

SUBJECT: ____________

MESSAGE ↑FOLD FOLD↑

SIGNED: ____________

REPLY

DATE: ____________

SIGNED: ____________

FORM NO. SKN1 HISTACOUNT CORPORATION, MELVILLE, N. Y. 11747

THIS COPY FOR PERSON ADDRESSED

Figure 8-2
A Typical Speedletter Form

4. Rubber Stamps

Brief, frequently used messages can be put on rubber stamps, which can be made to order at stationery stores for a few dollars. A number of these stamps are readily accessible if kept on a carousel. Pre-inked stamps save time in comparison with the less expensive type that have to be pressed onto an ink pad before each using.

Messages that can be covered by rubber stamps are ones like these:

> This item is no longer available. The closest substitute is our Cat. No. 2334. (*stamped at the bottom of an inquiry*)

Please send us copies of your brochure entitled:

Here is a copy of the literature you requested. (*stamped on the literature itself*)

5. Postcards

A postcard is faster and cheaper to prepare than a letter and envelope, requires less handling in the office, and goes at a lower postal rate, but still is handled as first-class mail. If postcards can be used frequently, one side can contain a color photo of your product or your office, or a sales message.

6. Telephone

A station-to-station telephone call halfway across the country, at the direct-dialed daytime rate, costs about $2.50, which is about half the cost of a dictated letter. In many cases the phone call is not only less expensive but also much more efficient in that the two-way communication provides an exchange of information that would take several letters to accomplish.

7. Telex

Although more expensive than a phone call, a telex message, especially to overseas points, usually produces a much speedier answer. If your volume would not justify your own telex equipment, consider using one of the telex service companies; they will handle your messages for you at a small markup over the routine telex charge.

8. Mailgrams

This cross between a letter and a telegram costs less than a telegram, more than a letter. It gets there faster than a letter. Since it resembles a telegram, it is usually used when getting the recipient's attention is important.

Other Ways to Save Money

Postage Meters

Even in a small office a postage meter can pay for itself. It saves the time often lost in hunting for stamps of infrequently used denominations; it saves money by reducing the likelihood that people will put on too much postage just because the smaller denomination stamp isn't handy or will "borrow" stamps for their personal correspondence.

Presorted First-Class Mail

First-class letters go at 2¢ less than the regular first-class rate if you can bundle ten or more letters going to the same five-digit zip code or 50 or more letters that have the same first three digits in the zip code.

Word Processors

These are great time-savers in handling not only routine and repetitive types of letters, but also more elaborate documents like proposals and contracts, which must be typed letter-perfect. Word processors are discussed in Chapter 16.

Dictating Equipment

Selection of the appropriate dictating equipment can save a great deal of staff time if the people who generate letters and reports dictate them rather than type their own rough drafts.

Dictating to an individual secretary or stenographer is probably the least efficient. It ties up the time of two persons instead of just one. If the person taking the dictation has other functions to perform, the dictation is an interruption that decreases efficiency in handling the other tasks. The work flow can be handled more smoothly when the "dictators" use some kind of recording device. In that way they can dictate whenever convenient to them, without waiting for a stenographer.

The commonest type of dictating equipment consists of an individual or "freestanding" piece of equipment that sits on the desk of the person doing the dictating or on a handy stand. It consists primarily of a microphone and a device that records the message on a belt, tape, or disk. The typist has a transcribing machine with foot pedal controls, to keep both hands free, and some means of backspacing.

One difficulty with the hand-held mike is that the person dictating often turns away from the mike to consult notes or reference material, and the recorded volume of the voice fades considerably. The typist has to listen to a phrase several times to decipher it. One study showed that the transcribing took 44% longer if the dictating was done into a hand-held mike as contrasted with a telephone-type instrument, which is automatically held in position in front of the mouth.

The other basic type of dictating equipment consists of a central recording device (Figure 8-3). A person wishing to dictate something dials an extension number on an interoffice phone line and dictates into the central equipment.

Earlier versions of this method consisted of a "tub" in which there was an endless loop of recording tape. Newer versions have a recorder that holds several tape cassettes. An advantage of this type is that it can

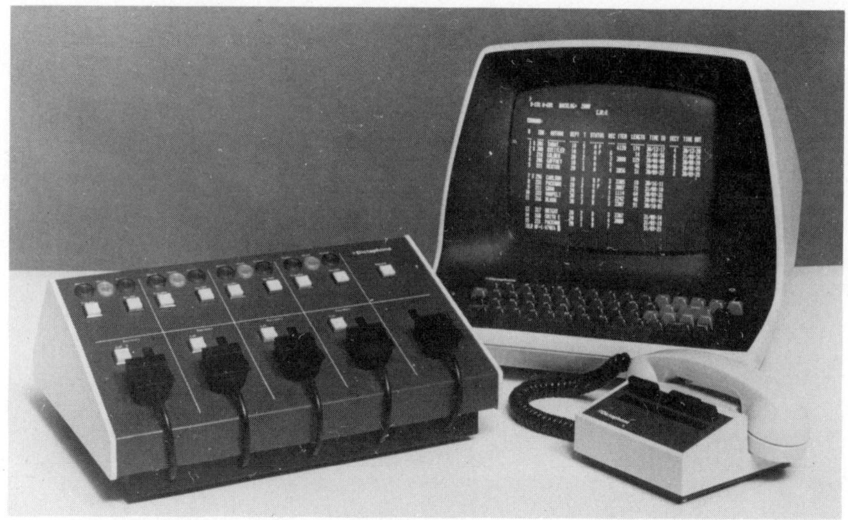

Figure 8-3
A Central Dictation Station—Dictaphone's "Thought Tank" System
(Courtesy Dictaphone Corporation, Rye, New York)

be programmed to start a new cassette after each 8 minutes of dictation—approximately an hour of typing. In that way the typing load can be evened out, or several typists can work on the same manuscript if it is a rush job.

Some of the telephone-type dictating machines enable a member of the staff to phone from outside the office and dial into or be connected with the dictating machine.

9
Reducing Telephone Costs

For most offices the telephone bill is the second or third largest item of expense. First come salaries, and next either rent or telephone.

While it may not be possible actually to reduce telephone costs, there are ways of minimizing their increase—which has the effect of reducing them as a percentage of expenses or income.

In this section we will discuss four ways of controlling telephone costs:

1. Buying your own equipment
2. Using a long-distance service
3. Auditing your phone bill occasionally
4. Holding down toll charges

BUYING YOUR OWN EQUIPMENT

Under the conventional contract with your local phone company you pay a monthly rental for every piece of phone equipment in the office: every extension, every button, every light on a button, everything. This rent goes on and on forever. It's like living in an apartment and paying rent on it all your life without ever owning it.

Until fairly recently it was illegal to hook up somebody else's equipment to telephone company lines. But recent court decisions required that the phone company attach its lines to your equipment, even if you provide your own equipment. This ruling has resulted in the establishment of a number of companies that sell and service telephone equipment.

In general, you can pay for the equipment over a 5-year (or other time) period. The annual payments are about the same as what you pay the phone company in rent, and at the end of 5 years you own the equipment—no more rent!

Most offices that have purchased their own equipment are happy with the service, but check it carefully before you make a commitment. Here are some of the steps in the decision:

1. Get a proposal from the phone company as well as from two or three suppliers of privately owned equipment. Some regional telephone companies offer similar purchase arrangements; even if they do not, you may find it more satisfactory to continue renting your equipment from the phone company.

2. Carefully check the background of the distributor of the telephone equipment. The equipment itself is manufactured in Japan, Sweden, or the United States but is installed and serviced by a local distributor. Get a credit rating on the distributor and check its background carefully; if the distributor goes out of business after your equipment is installed, you are in real trouble.

3. Get a list of all the users in your neighborhood (not just the names of a few satisfied customers the distributor is glad to give you), and check to see how fast the distributor provides service when something goes wrong.

4. Inquire about charges for service calls. If a phone goes dead, you cannot be sure whether the fault is in your equipment or in the telephone company's lines. If you phone the telephone company and they find that the fault is in the equipment, they will usually charge you for the service call. Some distributors of private equipment ask you to call them first and do not charge for the call if it develops that the fault is in the lines.

5. Check the provisions of the contract to see what happens if you want to change the equipment during the purchase period, trade it in for better equipment after it has been paid for, or move your office.

LONG-DISTANCE NETWORKS

The telephone company is facing increased competition from another direction. It is now legal for private companies to offer long-distance services by means of satellites and relay stations, at a cost per call about 30% less than AT&T charges. The major companies in this field are MCI, which uses the trade name "Execunet"; Southern Pacific Communications, with "Sprint"; Western Union; and U.S. Transmission Systems, Inc., a subsidiary of IT&T.

If you are a subscriber to one of these services, you dial a seven-digit local telephone number to get access to the long-distance network, dial a five-digit number that is your "password" and enables the system's computer to keep track of your charges, then dial the area code and seven-digit phone number you wish to reach.

If all this dialing sounds time-consuming (especially if the local access number is often busy), you can buy a gadget for about $100 that will automatically dial all 26 digits for you.

There is no initial charge (except for IT&T, which has a $10 charge), a nominal monthly minimum billing of $25 to $40, and no long-term contract to sign. You do need a Touch-Tone phone to dial into the system, although you can buy an adapter and continue to use the rotating dials.

One advantage of these services is that they give you a cost break on brief calls. AT&T charges for a minimum of 3 minutes and calculates your additional charge in increments of 1 minute; Sprint and MCI charge on a 30-second basis.

Points to consider in deciding whether to use such a service are the following:

1. These services do not cover all the area codes in North America. Each service will supply you with a map of the areas it covers. Compare it with your last month's record of outgoing long-distance calls to see if the network will cover most of your requirements.
2. Some subscribers complain about occasional noisy circuits. Check with users in your area to see how serious this is.
3. With Sprint, anyone anywhere in the country can use your code and call back into your office at the reduced rate—a capability worth considering if you have widely scattered salesmen or customers calling in.
4. Rates vary, too, as to whether you want a 24-hour service or one limited to office hours.

5. Primarily, take a month or two of your long-distance bills and see what you would save by using one of the networks. If you do most of your long-distance calling to suppliers' 800 (toll-free) numbers, the system may not be economical for you.

AUDITING YOUR TELEPHONE BILLS

There can be mistakes on your telephone bills, either as the result of deliberate fraud on somebody's part or as the result of billing errors. So it pays to check your phone bill—if not every month, at least occasionally.

There are three possible types of errors:

1. Local message unit calls may be charged to your phone by mistake. This does not happen too often, but the authors know of two office managers who thought their charges for local calls looked suspiciously high, checked with the phone company business office, and got the bills reduced.

2. Long-distance calls may have been charged to your phone or your credit card either mistakenly or as a result of deliberate fraud. Since all long-distance calls are itemized on your phone bill, it is not too difficult to check them occasionally, especially if you have your staff log their long-distance calls, as explained below.

3. Major overcharges can occur if you have changed your (rented) telephone equipment and the phone company mistakenly keeps charging you rent on the equipment that was removed. The first line on your monthly phone bill (see Figure 9-1) combines your basic monthly service charge with the total rental on all pieces of equipment. This rental charge is not itemized. If you have not done so recently, phone your local telephone business office and ask for an itemization of your bill. Check this against your actual equipment.

In many cities there are telephone consultants who will check your back phone bills at no charge, except that they get 50% of any refunds they collect on your behalf.

HOLDING DOWN TOLL CHARGES

1. Consider the use of an 800 (toll-free) number if you have customers or clients phoning you. The 800 number may cover only a small region or the entire country.

New York Telephone

914 738 1623 135 AUGUST 25 1981 PAGE 2

J PORTER HENRY JR BILL SUMMARY

PLEASE RETAIN THIS STATEMENT FOR YOUR RECORDS

PREVIOUS BILL	188.79	
PAYMENTS THRU AUG 27	188.79CR	
BALANCE DUE	.00	.00

MONTHLY SERVICE & EQUIPMENT AUG 25 THRU SEP 24	21.93	
OTHER CHARGES AND CREDITS- SEE DETAIL	.44	
LOCAL USAGE - SEE DETAIL	4.94	
DIRECTORY ASSISTANCE CREDIT @ .30 PER LINE	.30CR	
ITEMIZED CALLS - SEE DETAIL	33.11	
TAX-US 2% 1.20 S/L 5% 1.41	2.61	
CURRENT CHARGES INCLUDING TAXES	62.73	62.73

TOTAL AMOUNT DUE 62.73

TO DISCUSS YOUR BILL CALL YOUR REPRESENTATIVE 914 636-9950

Figure 9-1
A Typical Telephone Bill

2. Avoid excessive time charges on local calls. Although tariffs vary with each local phone company, in many cases local calls that cost two or more message units have a time charge after the first 3 or 4 minutes. Yet your staff members may believe that since it is a local call (within your own area code), there is no charge for additional minutes. Check the opening pages in your phone book; if this is the situation in your area, make sure that your people understand it.

3. Make all calls direct-dialed station-to-station calls. If one of your employees asks for any additional service, this is an "operator-assisted" call, which is billed at the full daily rate and carries an additional 50¢ charge. Such services include asking for time and charges, putting the call on a credit card, or asking that it be charged to another number.

4. Avoid person-to-person calls. The direct-dialed station calls are so much cheaper that you could make six or eight unsuccessful efforts to reach an important customer and still pay less than one person-to-person charge. If the customer is not in, you can always leave a callback message.

5. Call during reduced-rate periods. In the eastern part of the United States, let one employee stay after 5 P.M. to make all calls to time zones to the west. In the western part of the country, one employee can come in earlier to make accumulated calls to the east.

6. If you do have to make many outgoing calls at your own expense, give your staffers 3-minute egg timers and encourage them to hold their conversations to that time limit.

7. Make sure your staff uses the 800 numbers of suppliers wherever possible. Directories of 800 numbers are available; using them is probably faster than requesting the numbers from Directory Assistance. Each staff member should have a handy list of frequently used 800 numbers.

8. Regularly, or occasionally, have your employees keep a log of all the long-distance calls they make. You can provide a special form for the purpose, or they can simply keep a notebook on their desks and note the date, number called, and estimated length of time of each call.

You or a clerical person can check the logs against your phone bill at the end of the month to make sure they are using the least expensive method of reaching their parties and not making too many personal calls. As a means of controlling outgoing long-distance calls, some offices have one or two lines that do not tie in with the incoming lines, and they use only these for outgoing calls.

10

Office Layout and Space Management

An office is more than just a weatherproof environment for people, desks, and papers. It is a piece of communications equipment. Its function is to receive and process information, to make decisions on the basis of that information, and to manage the implementation of those decisions. Hence the key consideration in designing a new office, or rearranging an existing office, is to enable the staff to perform efficiently.

Yet this factor is often given inadequate attention in the design of a new office building. Jordan A. Berman of Jordan A. Berman Associates, Inc., in Boston, a leading consultant in office design, points out that the total cost of an office building over its lifetime consists of 2% construction costs, 6% to 8% maintenance costs, and 90% to 92% salary costs of the people who occupy it. Yet planners usually concentrate 85% to 90% of their efforts on the structure itself, which represents only 2% of the costs.

Looked at in another way, the space occupied by an experienced office employee costs about $1,800 a year, Berman reports, while the employee's salary and fringe benefits total about ten times that much. A 1% increase in workers' efficiency is as profitable as a 10% reduction in space costs.

WHAT GOES WHERE?

In a well-designed office, each person is as near as possible to the other persons he or she contacts frequently and to the files and other equipment used frequently.

A systematic way to locate people and equipment that minimizes walking from one place to another is to make an interaction analysis (Figure 10-1). In a large office the horizontal and vertical divisions would list the various departments: receiving, mail room, credit, sales office, personnel, bookkeeping, and so on. In a smaller office the divisions might include names of individuals as well as frequently used equipment like the office copier, central files, and credit records.

During the course of a typical week, each employee keeps a log of the number of times he or she physically travels to another office or piece

	Owner/manager	Owner's sec'y	Receptionist/ mail handler/filing	Typist	Bookkeeper	Artist/layout	Sales mgr.	Sales rep.	Service person	Central files	Copier	Ref. books/catalogs	Supply closet
Owner/manager		68	21	8	9	7	28	14	10	2	4	8	2
Owner's secretary	68		32	18	11	14	16	12	12	10	12	16	6
Receptionist/ mail handler/filing	21	32		12	15	8	29	7	11	103	20	35	17
Typist	8	18	12		4	6	25	12	14	30	18	16	12
Bookkeeper	9	11	15	4		3	12	6	11	7	4	8	8
Artist/layout	7	14	8	6	3		22	13	4	6	12	5	9
Sales mgr.	28	16	29	25	12	22		35	25	10	7	4	3
Sales rep.	14	12	7	12	6	13	35		21	15	9	8	4
Service person	10	12	11	14	11	4	25	21		3	2	6	4
Central files	2	10	103	30	7	6	10	15	3				
Copier	4	12	20	18	4	12	7	9	2				
Ref. books/catalogs	8	16	35	16	8	5	4	8	6				
Supply closet	2	6	17	12	8	9	3	4	4				

Figure 10-1

"Interaction Chart." Chart shows interoffice contacts and equipment usage for a week. Each person should be next to the two or three persons or things contacted most frequently.

of equipment. These contacts are totalled, as shown in Figure 10-1, and the name of the game is to put each department or person next to the two or three most frequently contacted departments or objects.

WORK STATIONS

For each individual in the office (or, in a larger organization, for each group of individuals performing similar tasks) the planner needs to determine what is needed at that work station. The needs usually consist of:

1. Work surface or surfaces (How big?)
2. Reference materials and records
3. Storage space, including personal storage—coats, purses, umbrellas
4. Space for equipment like a typewriter, word processor, or computer
5. Space for supplies like typewriting paper
6. Communications needs: telephone equipment, any other equipment like Telex, TWX, etc.
7. Any needs for privacy
8. Acoustical and lighting needs

WHAT BASIC DESIGN?

The office planner has a choice of three basic types of offices:

1. Walled-off private offices
2. Offices separated by semi-partitions
3. An open office, without partitions of any kind

These types are often mixed; for example, the executives may have private offices with all the support personnel in an open area.

Pros and cons of the three types are as follows.

Private Offices

These provide maximum privacy. Writers in offices of magazines or advertising agencies may feel they can be more productive in closed offices, although newspapermen long ago learned to work in an open city room environment. Private offices cost more to heat, light, and air condition than the same square footage of open space. Another disadvantage is that the arrangement is not very flexible when there are personnel changes.

Semi-Partitions

This arrangement gives an impression of greater airiness and spaciousness than walled-in offices of the same size. The chest-high semi-partitions provide some element of privacy, and yet the manager can be aware of what is going on in the office.

Open Environment

This makes for easy communication from one desk to another—too easy, in some cases. Offices performing a sales function, such as life insurance agencies, real estate firms, and travel agencies, often find that it is easier to close the sale in a semi-partitioned environment. Prospects seem more willing to ask questions and make decisions when there is some semblance of privacy.

HANDLING VISITORS

The layout of an office is influenced by the frequency of visits by clients or customers. If people are coming into your office to avail themselves of your services, as is the case with a real estate office or travel agency, the layout may be substantially different from that of an office with infrequent visitors.

If your office is essentially a service point for customers or clients, you will naturally want an attractive reception area where they can indicate their requirements and where they can wait comfortably if waiting is necessary. A coffee table may offer a selection of current magazines or perhaps literature such as catalogs or brochures that will explain your services or might help the client predetermine his or her interests.

There are basically two kinds of layouts for offices which service clients:

1. The "open access" layout (Figure 10-2), in which a client walking through the door has access to every desk and merely walks up to the staff member who is not already engaged.
2. The "traffic control" layout (Figure 10-3), in which the entering customer first meets a receptionist or "fast service" counter.

In a smaller office the person who greets the customer is usually not a full-time receptionist, but one who greets customers and routes incoming phone calls while handling other secretarial or clerical duties. This receptionist is usually one of the newer and less expensive employees.

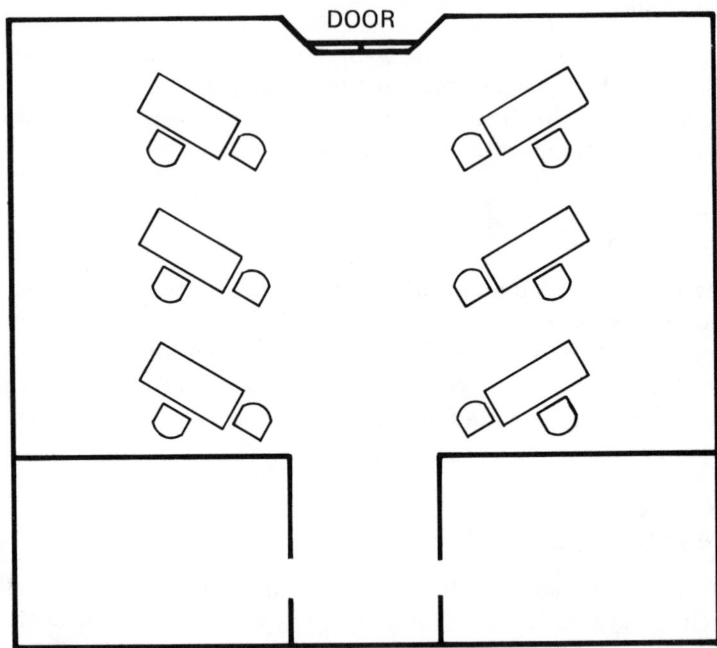

Figure 10-2
An "Open" Layout: Customers or Visitors Can Walk up to Any Desk

He or she handles simple requests and refers more complicated questions to the appropriate experienced employee.

The open layout is satisfactory where there is not too much walk-in traffic, as in offices on an upper floor of an office building. But for street-level offices in a business district or mall, the controlled access layout is usually more efficient.

PLANNING THE LAYOUT

The easiest way for amateur office planners to experiment with various placements of people and furniture is to use squared paper (you can make copies of Figure 10-4 if you wish) to make a layout of floor space. A handy scale to work with is to have ¼ inch on the paper (one of the squares) represent 1 foot of floor space.

Trace the dimensions of your office on the squared paper. Then make paper cutouts, to scale, representing chairs, desks, tables, file cabinets, etc., and move them around until you get the most efficient arrangement.

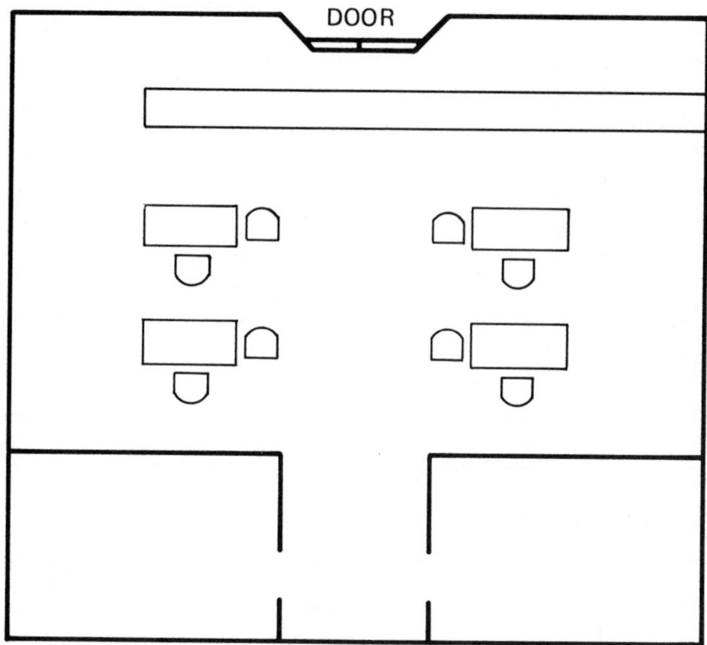

Figure 10-3
A "Traffic Control" Layout: Visitors Are Screened at the Counter

There are some other basic considerations that you should take into account. Should the manager have a private office with solid walls, or a semiprivate enclosure with chest-high walls so the manager can see the activities in the office, or should the manager simply have a desk in an open area? Do you need a conference room? If it would be used infrequently, consider making the manager's office large enough, with a table and a few extra chairs, so that it can be used for an occasional conference.

Primarily, you want to make each person's work station as complete as possible, so that he or she can perform most tasks without leaving the desk. If there is some file or equipment that individuals do have to walk to, it should be centrally located with respect to those who use it.

This suggests that files used by the entire staff should be near the center of the office, and so should the water fountain and the coffee maker, unless you provide a separate area for coffee breaks and luncheons.

If the files are near the center of the office, they can be painted in attractive colors, used as area dividers, or dressed up with a plant or figurine on top, rather than a jumble of reference books and documents.

Noisy equipment like bookkeeping machines should be relegated to an enclosure at the rear, or even to another floor. Street-level offices some-

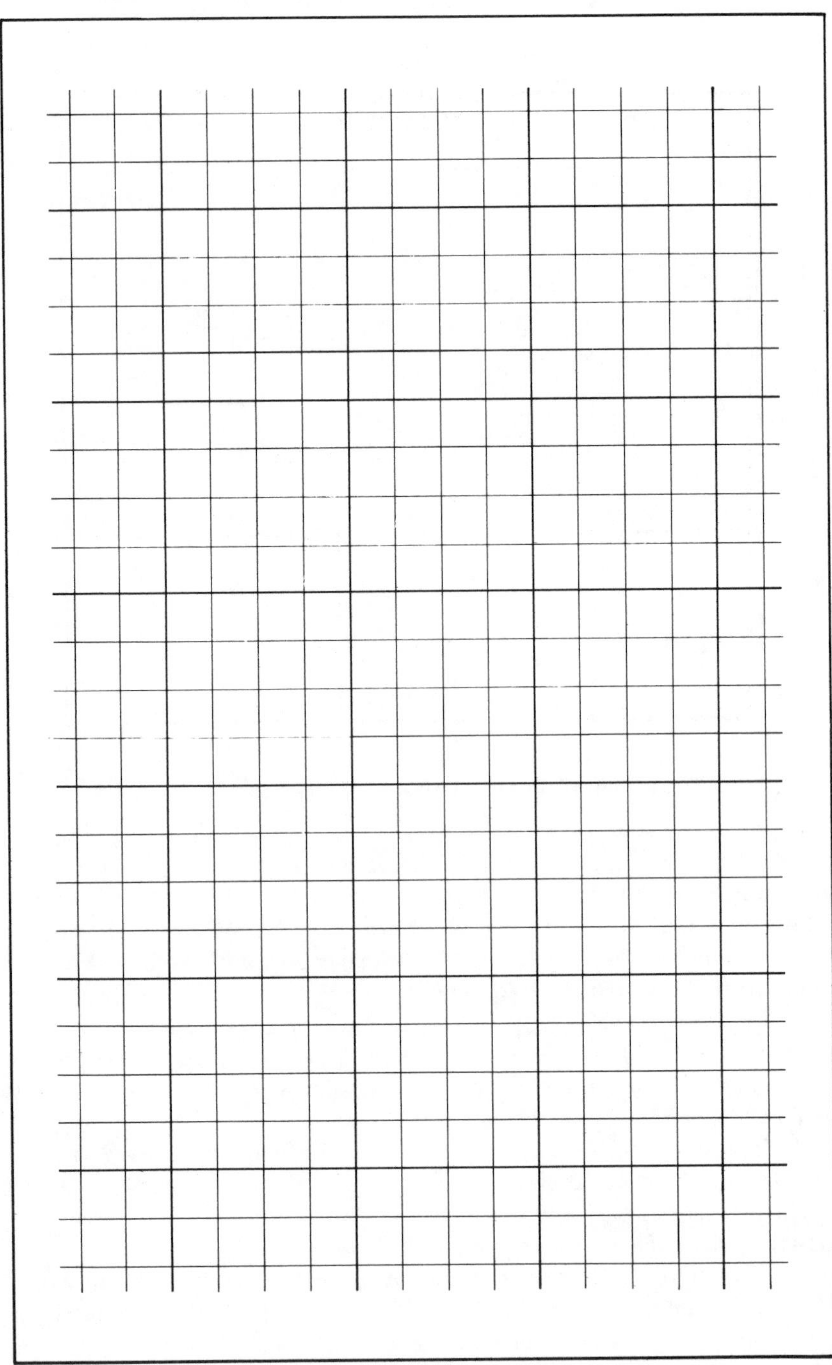

Figure 10-4
Squared Paper for Layout

times have basement space available. This equipment area, wherever it is, should be especially well lighted.

Give some thought to noise control, especially where each desk is used for typing. An office need not sound like a boiler factory. Acoustical tile on the ceiling, commercial grade carpet on the floors, bookcases, even plants, all help to absorb noise.

Try whenever possible to have paperwork flow in a straight line, rather than going forward, sideways, then back. Incoming mail, for example, should move in a straight line from the person who opens it, to the person who receives and handles it, to the mailing desk and files.

If one set of files or one piece of equipment needs to be used frequently by two or three employees, consider putting it on a "lazy Susan," which enables each person to spin it around to get access to it.

Do not let surplus or obsolete furniture take up valuable office space. Empty file cabinets, unused chairs, outdated literature, and the like should be junked or moved to dead storage.

Provide a minimum of 40 footcandles of light on the surfaces of desks. Be sure to minimize glare, which is more fatiguing than most people realize. Lighting engineers say that in an environment with considerable glare, 50% of the body's muscular energy is absorbed by the constant adjustments of the eyes.

There are basically two kinds of glare: direct glare and reflected glare. Direct glare occurs when the light source can shine directly into a person's eyes. This is eliminated by using lenses or diffusers on light fixtures.

Reflected glare is sometimes more difficult to control. Desk tops should not be covered with glass or any other shiny material that reflects ceiling lights; matte finishes are preferred. The modern tendency is to provide localized "task" lighting on each job and rely less on general room lighting. Another source of indirect glare is too much contrast between the surface of the desk and the documents being worked on. If the desk surface is dark and the papers on it are white, the eyes are fatigued by the constant adjustments required as they move from one area to another.

CHECKING YOUR PRESENT LAYOUT

Can you eliminate unnecessary steps just by rearranging your present furniture? A good way to answer that question is to draw a floor plan, as described earlier in this chapter, with all the furniture in place. Lay a transparent sheet over it—you can buy acetate sheets at art stores—and with a colored pen trace the steps one employee must take to and from the necessary files, supplies, or equipment. Using different colors, repeat the process for other employees.

Then study the map of footprints to see where some of the walking could be eliminated by rearranging furniture. Make a floor plan of your new layout, place a transparency over it, and again trace the footsteps of each staff member. (You might use a separate transparency for each staffer.) This is a way of making sure that you have not increased one person's traveling while cutting down on someone else's.

11

Policies and Procedures Manuals

It makes sense for even the smallest of organizations to develop a policies and procedures manual. Such a manual is a great time-saver. It is cumbersome to make a policy decision each time the same question arises, when it could be decided in a jiffy by consulting the manual.

The "policies" portion covers the firm's policies in such matters as vacation, sick leave, severance pay, fringe benefits, and the like. It prevents future misunderstandings with the employees by spelling everything out in advance. Some offices give new employees a copy of the manual, go through it with them, and have them sign it.

The "procedures" part establishes the standard procedures for tasks like opening and distributing mail, handling incoming cash and checks, handling correspondence, and filing. It is useful in training new employees, and it helps keep repetitive operations handled in the most efficient way.

A suggested outline for a policies and procedures manual appears at the end of this chapter. This is merely a starting point; each reader will delete some topics and add others.

How do you get the manual written? Bring the staff into the act. The manager will probably write the first draft of the policies portion, then circulate it to see if there are any questions it does not cover. As to the procedures portion, why not let the employee who is most familiar with each procedure write the first draft description of that procedure? It, too, can be circulated among those who perform each described function to see if they can make any corrections or improvements.

For most small offices a typewritten manuscript in a ring binder is adequate. Revisions to such a manual are easy. A word processor is useful because the manual can be stored in its memory. When there is a change, that portion can be corrected, printed out, reproduced, and distributed. When a new employee is added, it is simple enough to print out an extra copy of the entire manuscript.

OUTLINE OF POSSIBLE CONTENTS

Part One: Policies

I. Company background
   A. History and description
   B. Management structure; organization chart
   C. Job descriptions
II. New employees
   A. Probation period
   B. Duties; expected achievement
   C. Method of evaluation
III. Training programs
   A. On-the-job training
   B. Staff meetings
   C. Self-study programs
   D. Outside training
   E. Assistance in educational programs
IV. Part-time and temporary employees
V. Full-time employees
   A. Promotion policies
   B. Transfers to other departments
   C. Layoffs
   D. Resignations
   E. Discharges
VI. Compensation
   A. Basic compensation
   B. Profit-sharing or incentive plan
   C. Merit raises
   D. Cost-of-living adjustments
   E. Overtime
VII. Benefits
   A. Vacation
   B. Sick leave
   C. Emergency leave

D. Maternity leave
E. Pension plan
F. Medical plan

Part Two: Procedures

I. Incoming mail
  A. Opening and distributing
  B. Policies on correspondence marked "Personal"
  C. Material to be circulated "FYI" and then filed
II. Outgoing mail
  A. Persons responsible for each type
  B. Use of form letters, standardized letter formats, etc.
  C. Postage or postage meters
  D. Handling of packages: which go parcel post, UPS, air express, etc.
III. Incoming money
  A. Handling incoming cash and checks
  B. Bookkeeping and accounting procedures
  C. Deposits
IV. Accounts payable
  A. Approval of invoices
  B. Payment
  C. Bookkeeping procedures
V. Filing
  A. List of files, with materials filed in each
  B. Filing procedures
  C. Procedures for removing and refiling items
  D. Records retention schedules and responsibility
VI. Purchasing
  A. Authority for various types and sizes of purchases
  B. Selection of vendors or requests for bids
  C. Purchase orders
  D. Payment
  E. Petty cash

Part Three

MORE EFFICIENT EQUIPMENT

12

Equipment Decisions: Buy, Lease, or Do Without?

Throughout this part of the book we will be looking at various kinds of equipment designed to enable the office staff to get its work done in less time—equipment like computers, word processors, and copying machines.

At what point does it make sense to acquire a particular piece of equipment? And if it does make sense, should you buy it or lease it? The primary questions you need to answer are:

1. How much staff time will this equipment save?
2. What is the cost of this staff time?
3. Would the cost of buying or leasing the equipment be more or less than the cost of the staff time it saves?

Rarely in a small office would you actually be able to reduce the size of the staff. But if you are spending $100 a week in staff time on some manual operation that could be done electronically with one third the staff time, you are spending $67 a week in processing time that could perhaps be applied to more important or more profitable tasks.

The saving in staff time is usually the primary consideration, but it may not be the only one. Greater accuracy and a more favorable impression on customers are intangibles you may also want to consider in making your decision.

THE "DECISION TABLE"

Table 12-1 illustrates the basic factors involved in making the decision; it can easily be modified to fit specific types of equipment.

1. Annual Cost of Staff Time

How many hours a week is it taking the staff to handle the process manually? (You can base your calculations on weekly costs, monthly costs, or annual costs. Staff hours are usually easiest to calculate on a weekly basis. But since lease costs are usually quoted in months, your final comparison will often be on a monthly basis. To convert weekly costs to monthly costs, multiply by $4\frac{1}{3}$, not by 4.) How many hours a week would it take the staff to do the same job with the contemplated equipment? Usually, the cost of staff time will be much lower with the automated equipment.

Table 12-1
Elements in the Lease-or-Buy Decision

	Without the Equipment	*With the Equipment*	
		Leased	*Purchased*
1. Annual cost of staff time	Highest	Lower	Lower
2. Owning cost	None	Annual cost of lease	Amount of investment written off each year, plus interest on one-half the total cost.
3. Maintenance cost	None	Usually included in the lease	Cost of annual maintenance contract, or estimated cost of spot repairs
4. Per-unit operating costs	None	?	?
5. Other costs: a. Installation b. Power c. Space	None	?	?
6. TOTAL COSTS:	?	?	?
Less tax savings on write-off	?	?	?
NET COSTS	?	?	?

2. Owning Cost

How much would it cost you to have the piece of equipment in your office? If you lease the equipment, the owning cost is the annual cost of the lease. If you buy the equipment, your owning cost is the sum of two components:

1. The amount of capital written off each year. For example, if you pay $5,000 for a microcomputer and write off the cost in 3 years, the capital cost is $1,667 per year.

2. Interest on capital invested. During the period in which the equipment is written off, you have, on the average, half the cost tied up in capital invested. Multiply that figure by the current interest rate. For example, you buy a copying machine for $1,200 and write it off in 4 years. On the average, during the 4-year period, you have $600 of your capital not yet written off, but tied up in the equipment. For example, $600 × 18% is $106 a year, the interest cost of the average amount of capital invested in the equipment. Even if you have the purchase money and do not need to borrow it, you still add in the capital cost; if you had not spent the money for the copier, you could have invested it at interest.

In Table 12-1 we assumed that you have no equipment costs in your present manual operation. This is not always true; often you are comparing the cost of a simple piece of manual equipment with a more expensive automated version. For example, in considering the lease or purchase of a word processor, your present costs would include the owning and maintenance costs on the manual typewriter now being used.

3. Maintenance Costs

How much per year will it cost you to keep the equipment in operating order? If you lease it, maintenance and repairs are usually included in the lease. If not, or if you buy the equipment, you need to:

1. determine the cost of an annual flat-rate maintenance contract, or
2. make a generous allowance for possible costs of repairs paid for as needed.

4. Per-Unit Operating Costs

Is there any cost or charge for each item processed? Leased office copying machines are often metered to charge the user a few cents for each copy run off. Travel agents pay 10¢ for airline tickets printed out by the computer connected to an airline. If you buy a copier, there is usually a cost per copy for special papers, inks, or toners.

5. Other Costs

Depending upon the type of equipment being considered, you may wish to enter other costs of the type listed under this heading in Table 12-1.

6. Total

Add up the columns. The lowest total indicates the decision that should be the most profitable for your office, with two important exceptions:

1. You may want to choose a more expensive alternative if it will improve customer relations or enhance your office's image.

2. In considering highly technical equipment in a rapidly changing field, like computers and word processors, it is usually advisable to lease rather than buy, even if leasing is a bit more expensive. Reason: Technology is changing so rapidly that the piece of equipment you purchase may be obsolete before you finish paying for it.

AN EXAMPLE

To illustrate this decision process, let's take a childishly simple example (Table 12-2). A small office has no copying machine of its own. "When we need a copy of anything," the manager explains, "one of the employees goes to a copying place just around the corner, and they run it off for a dime."

The first step in almost any decision involving efficiency is to analyze the present situation. The manager keeps a log for a week or two and finds that, on the average, an employee goes out to get a copy 36 times a week and that it takes an average of 8 minutes each time. If the cost of staff time is 14¢ a minute, the costs under the present system, as shown in the first column of Table 12-2, would be:

Staff time, 8 minutes × 36 × $0.14	$40.32
Operating costs, $0.10 × 36 copies	3.60
TOTAL COSTS, doing without	$43.92

Now let's say that the manager can lease a copier for $50 a month plus 3½ cents per copy. With the copier right in the office, it would take

Table 12-2
Equipment Decision on Office Copier
(weekly costs, 36 copies)

	Doing Without	*Leasing*	*Buying*
Staff time			
at 8 min. each	$40.32		
at 1 min. each		$ 5.04	$ 5.04
Owning cost	none		
Lease		12.50	
Purchase			7.55
Operating cost	3.60	1.26	.72
Maintenance	none	(included)	4.00
Totals	$43.92	$18.80	$17.31

only 1 minute of staff time to run off a copy. Maintenance and supplies are included in the lease. So the total costs if a copier is leased would be:

Staff time, 1 minute × 36 × $0.14	$ 5.04
Lease cost per week, approx.	12.50
Operating costs, $0.035 × 36 copies	1.26
TOTAL COSTS, leasing	$18.30

Suppose the manager can buy a copier for $1,000. If the manager depreciates it in 3 years, capital is being written off at the rate of $333 a year or $6.40 per week. On the average, during the lifetime of the copier, half of its cost is tied up in capital. That is $500; and if the interest rate is 12%, the value of that capital is $60 a year, or $1.15 a week. So the total owning costs are $7.55 a week.

The manager can get a maintenance contract from the supplier for $200 a year, or $4 per week. Supplies of the special paper needed cost 2¢ per copy, or 72¢ per week. So the total cost if the manager buys the equipment would be:

Staff time, 36 minutes × $0.14	$ 5.04
Owning cost	7.55
Maintenance	4.00
Operating cost	0.72
TOTAL COST, purchasing	$17.31

Hence in this very hypothetical example it would be more economical to buy the equipment than to lease it or do without it.

13

Computers in General

With microcomputers available for as little as $600 or so, for most small offices the question is not "Computer: yes or no?" but more likely, "A computer, yes—but how soon and what kind?"

There are three ways in which a small office can automate some of its paperwork processing:

1. It can use a service bureau. This is a company that owns its own computer and uses it to process data like payrolls, financial statements, and accounts receivable of its clients.

2. It can use time sharing. Here again the supplier owns a large computer. Its customers have small computer consoles, like portable typewriters, which connect to the big computer by telephone wires.

3. It can buy or lease its own "freestanding" computer.

More about these questions later. Let's first take a quick layperson's look at how computers work.

THE ABC'S OF COMPUTERS

The technical name for the use of computers is "electronic data processing," usually shorted to EDP. A computer, in other words, is a device that takes data—financial information, payroll records, mathematical formulas—and processes it electronically. Computers work at fantastic speeds. They can complete one basic calculation in a "nanosecond"—one-thousandth of one-millionth (one-billionth) of a second.

How long do you think it would take a computer to perform all of these calculations?

- Debit 2,000 checks to 300 different bank accounts.
- Examine the electrocardiograms of 100 patients and alert their physicians to possible trouble.
- Score 150,000 answers on 3,000 examinations and calculate the grades.
- Compute the payroll for a company with 1,000 employees.

A large computer could perform all those calculations in half a second! Of course, it could not print the bank statements and paychecks that rapidly, but it could do all the necessary arithmetic in that fraction of a second.

As to reliability, a computer ordinarily will make an error less than 0.005 of 1% of the time—one calculation out of 500,000. Further, many computers have a built-in error-detecting capacity, which signals that something is wrong. Most computer errors are caused by mistakes in feeding the data into the computer.

A computer system consists essentially of three parts:

1. Some kind of input device to feed the data into the computer: a typewriterlike keyboard, magnetic cards, magnetic disks, or whatever
2. The computer itself
3. Some kind of output device, to print the results in the form of statements or paychecks, or to store the processed data for future use

Let's first take a more detailed look at the computer itself. The computer, with all its circuits and memory cells, is called the "hardware" of the EDP system. The word "software" is used to describe the programs that tell the computer how to process the data it receives.

Every computer has some kind of built-in memory, or "storage." The larger the computer, the larger its internal memory. However, no computer is big enough to store in its internal memory all the data it will be working with, so additional outside or "auxiliary" memory is provided in the form of tapes or disks.

There are two ways in which items stored in an external memory can be reached, or "accessed": "random access" and "sequential access."

In random access the computer can go immediately to the desired information, without having to run through all the data that precedes it in the memory. It is something like a phonograph record; if you want to hear a portion of it in the middle, you can simply place the needle on that spot without having to play all the preceding music.

In sequential access the computer must search through the data in sequence, from the beginning up to the desired bit of data. It is something like a tape recorder. If you want to hear a selection in the middle of the tape, you have to run through the preceding tape—"fast forward," it's true, but the tape still has to pass the recording head in sequence.

Digital computers, the kind we will be talking about, really have only a two-word vocabulary: "ON" and "OFF." Thousands of tiny magnetic cores are either magnetized (ON) or demagnetized (OFF). The computer reads ON as 1 and OFF as 0.

Since it has only 1 and 0 to work with, the computer cannot count 1, 2, 3, 4, . . . as we do in our decimal (meaning "to-the-base-10") system. Instead it uses the binary (to-the-base-2) system, like this:

"Our numbers" (decimal)		*"Computer numbers" (binary)*
1	=	1
2	=	10
3	=	11
4	=	100
5	=	101
6	=	110
7	=	111
8	=	1000
9	=	1001
10	=	1010
11	=	1011
12	=	1100
13	=	1101
14	=	1110
15	=	1111
16	=	10000
.		.
.		.
.		.

Each ON/OFF position is called a "bit," short for "binary digit." Most small computers work with groups of eight binary digits. This group is called a "byte." The size of the computer's internal memory is measured in thousands of bytes. Computer people use the letter "K" to stand for 1,000; it is the initial of the Greek word "kilo" for 1,000.

Computers are divided rather loosely into three basic categories:

1. Microcomputers, for home and small office use, are designed to handle relatively small amounts of data, with comparatively slow speeds of processing and printing. Their memories range from 4K to 32K; they cost from $500 to about $5,000.

2. Minicomputers have larger memories and faster speeds. They cost from $5,000 to $25,000.

3. Full-size computers have large memories and can calculate and print at lightning speeds—up to 1,500 lines per minute as compared with about 50 lines per minute for the home microcomputers.

The computer's internal memory is used in three ways (Figure 13-1):

1. The permanent instruction, "wired" into the computer by the manufacturer, which tells the computer where to store each bit of data, how to follow the programmed instructions, and so on.

2. The program that the computer is currently running. For example, if it is calculating the payroll, the payroll program, which is stored on disks or tapes, must be "dumped" into the computer's internal memory. This program instructs the computer to take each employee's number, print the number of hours he or she worked, multiply it by that person's hourly rate, take off the specified deductions, write out a paycheck, and update the master file.

3. The data on which the computer is working. In the case of the payroll this would include a list of the employees' names and numbers, the hours each one worked, hourly rate, deduction information, and so on.

When the computer has finished working on a program, the program itself and the updated data are taken out of the computer and stored in the auxiliary memory.

In addition to its storage, or memory, the computer contains two other segments (Figure 13-1):

1. The control unit. This runs through the program, step by step, "telling" the logic unit at each step what to do with each bit of data.
2. The arithmetic logic unit, which performs the calculations.

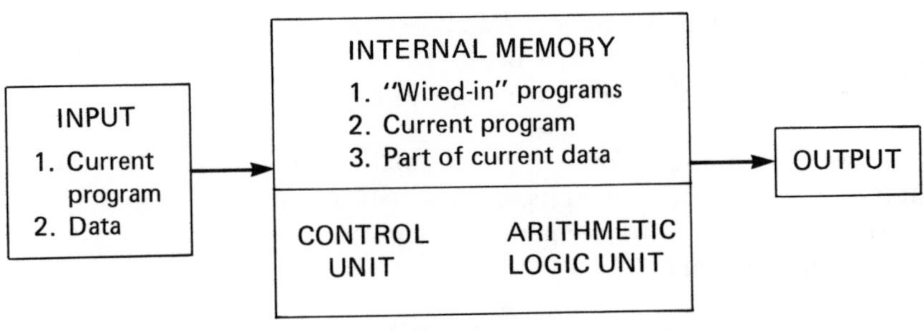

Figure 13-1
Elements of a Computer

COMPUTER PROGRAMS

A program is a piece of software that tells the computer, step by step, what to do with the data it is working on. It is much like the recipe for baking a cake:

- Step one: Take out an egg.
- Step two: Crack it.
- Step three: Open the shell.
- Step four: Let the white drip into a bowl.
- Step five: Put the yoke in another bowl.
- LOOP: Repeat steps 1 through 5 five more times.

The small business computer needs a program for each function it is supposed to perform. There are two ways of obtaining these programs:

1. You can buy "ready-made" programs, known as "commercial software." There are on the market hundreds of programs for such functions as payroll, accounts receivable, general ledger, and mailing lists. The cost of programs for small businesses ranges from about $75 to $2,000. Usually, the program must be designed or modified for the particular make of computer on which it is to be used.
2. If you need some very special program, you can write your own or hire a professional programmer to do it for you.

COMPUTER LANGUAGES

Naturally, the computer cannot understand a language; it can't even understand the letter "A" unless it has been translated into the computer's binary bits. But computer experts have designed languages that you can use to tell the computer what to do. Some of the languages are rather complicated and mathematical, but some of the newer ones are mostly in English. The most commonly used computer languages are:

- BASIC: a simple program language in which you simply type into the computer instructions like "RUN," "LIST," "IF X > 20 GOTO LINE 500," and so on.
- RPG (for Report Program Generator): a fairly simple language for pulling reports out of a file.
- COBOL (for COmmon Business Oriented Language): a language developed in 1959 by Grace Hopper of the Navy Management Office. It was the first computer language to use English words like MOVE, READ, COMPARE, ADD. It is used primarily for business applications like accounting and payroll. It is fairly easy to learn.
- FORTRAN (for FORmula TRANslation): a language developed by IBM in 1957, designed primarily for scientific, mathematical, and engineering applications. It has been modified over the years; the current version is FORTRAN IV.
- PL/1: a combination of FORTRAN and COBOL, with some distinctive characteristics of its own.

Microcomputers use BASIC; minicomputers usually use RPG or COBOL; full-sized computers usually use FORTRAN, COBOL, or PL/1.

INPUT DEVICES

Keyboard

This is the input device most commonly used in small business applications. The computer has a keyboard with letters and numbers arranged like those on a typewriter keyboard; some computers also have a separate array of numbers arranged like those on a calculator for faster input of numerical data. There is almost always a CRT (cathode-ray tube) like a television screen so the operator can see the data while typing it in.

Direct Input from Business Machines

In a retail or wholesale establishment, for example, cash registers or computer terminals that handle individual transactions can be connected directly to the computer, so that each transaction is automatically recorded for purpose of billing, inventory control, and financial records.

Punch Cards

The standard card has 80 vertical columns, with 12 characters in each column. Letters and numbers are represented by punching out two of the digits in each column. This is normally done on a keypunch machine, although if the volume of cards is too small to justify the purchase of such a machine, "portapunch" cards can be punched by hand. The holes on these cards have been partially die-cut and can be punched out with a stylus.

Data from the input documents is transferred from the paper documents to the cards by a keypunch operator and then fed into the computer by a card reader. This device passes a series of metal brushes over the card. Where a hole has been punched out, the brush closes an electrical circuit and reads the digit.

The principal disadvantage of punch cards is the time required to transfer the information to the cards manually and then check them for accuracy. If cards are retained, they also take up considerable storage space.

Magnetic Tape

The tape has metal dots on it, comparable to the location of the holes in a punch card. Data can be transferred to tape by means of a typewriter keyboard, or it can be read onto the tape from punch cards by means of a card reader.

Magnetic Disks

These are disks that look like a phonograph record. The surface has a coating that can be magnetized so that data can be transferred to the disks in the usual ON/OFF computer language. *Magnetic cards* or "mag cards" work in the same way.

Optical Scanner

This device enables the computer to actually "see" letters and numbers if they are printed in a characteristic block fashion—like account numbers on your bank checks. The document is passed under a light ray that is reflected back onto a photocell where there is no mark but is absorbed where there is a mark. The computer compares the pattern it sees with a built-in "vocabulary" of patterns and translates them into words or numbers. The series of lines on food packages is an example of a pattern that is scanned optically by a computer at the checkout counter.

COMPUTER SYSTEMS

There are two kinds of computer systems:

1. Interactive, in which the user operates a small computer, or a console connected to a larger computer, and can ask questions or get the results immediately.
2. Batch processing, in which some type of data, such as orders, is accumulated and then done in a batch when the computer is not otherwise occupied. This is less expensive, because a slower computer can be used. Batch processing is usually best for a small business; it can process all its orders at one time, then all its invoice, and so on.

Figure 13-2 summarizes the elements of EDP systems in general. Figure 13-3 illustrates a typical example: payroll processing.

THE RANGE OF COMPUTER APPLICATIONS

We commonly think of a computer as a data processor, handling information about payrolls, sales, and orders. But there are many other computer applications.

1. Filing, processing, and retrieving information. This is the application most familiar in the small office. All kinds of data can be stored in the auxiliary memory, updated, and processed. When desired, the data can be pulled up into the CRT or printed on paper, cards, or microfilm. When used in this manner, the computer is serving as an electronic filing cabinet." There are two types of retrieval:
   a. Record retrieval of a specific bit of information. For example, "Go through the file of purchasing orders and show me Purchase Order No. 95484."
   b. Data retrieval of some class of information. For example, "Search all of last year's purchase orders and print out all those over $500 from the state of California." Types of data stored include personnel records, purchases, sales, credit information, customer records, inventory, and payrolls.
2. Manipulation of data. The information can be converted to charts, graphs, or tables. The charts of individual stock performances distributed by investment advisory services are all prepared by computers.
3. Simulation. A program is created by which the computer can simulate the operation of a sales force, a rapid transit system, a factory, a retail store. The user can then ask "what if—?" questions: 'What would happen if I added two more salespeople?" "What will happen to my net profits if my rent increases by 10%?"

SOURCE DOCUMENT (readable by humans)	CONVERTED TO LANGUAGE THE COMPUTER CAN READ	COMPUTER'S CENTRAL PROCESSING UNIT	DATA OUTPUT (in a form readable by humans)	EXTERNAL STORAGE
Time card Purch. order Invoice Shipping records etc.	Keyboard Punch cards Optical pattern Magnetic card, tape, disk	The program of instructions That part of the data being processed	CRT display Documents: Checks Reports Microfilm	Master files

Figure 13-2
Schematic Diagram of Data Processing

INPUT	DATA ENTRY	PROCESSING	OUTPUT	STORAGE
Time card with employee's no. and hours worked	Keyboard	Multiply hours worked by hourly rate, subtract deductions (up to a limit), and withhold tax	Pay checks Payroll register and reports: by dept. by week or month amount of overtime pay, etc.	Master employee record Names, numbers Rate of pay Dependents, deductions

Figure 13-3
Payroll Processing as an EDP Example

4. Process control. A computer can be integrated into a manufacturing process to control temperature, pressure, proportions of various elements in a mix, and so on. Oil refineries are operated almost entirely by computers. Computers that control processes are usually analog computers—they sense the gradations between one number and the next instead of going from one discrete number (however small) to the next. Business computers are usually digital computers—their input is in the form of digits like "56" or digital fractions like "5.948." An analog computer is something like a slide rule; a digital computer is more like a pocket calculator.
5. Pattern recognition. An example is the pattern of wide and narrow bars that appears on supermarket packages. This pattern is the "Uniform Product Code" and can be optically interpreted by a microcomputer, which not only prices each item and adds up the customer's check, but also uses the data for inventory control and financial records. Optical pattern recognition is practical when large masses of data must be fed into the computer. It is used in processing direct mail returns and in handling the "cents off" coupons turned in at supermarkets.
6. Mathematical calculations. In addition to the ordinary arithmetic operations of a small business, a computer can be programmed to perform complicated mathematical calculations. For example, a computer can calculate the square root of 2 out to 100 decimal places in a fraction of a second, something that would take hours to do manually.
7. Problem solving. A computer can be programmed to solve complicated problems, such as playing chess. This capability enables it to check the accuracy of research reports, for example.
8. Word processing. The computer can act as a "typewriter with a memory." This is covered in Chapter 16.
9. Computer graphics. The computer can be used to "draw pictures." These might be graphs, like curves showing trends in prices, or physical objects. A computer can take a blueprint of an object and project it on the screen as it would be seen from any desired angle; it can even rotate the image on the screen.

A study of computer applications made by Honeywell indicated that these were the most common:

1. For small business:
   a. Payroll and accounting. These are the easiest to dump onto a computer, either through "canned" software or by means of a service bureau. Using them enables the small office to make a start at automation and gain confidence in it.

   b. Personnel records, including pension plan data, employee records, and employee experience.
   c. General accounting. There are hundreds of available software packages for general ledger, accounts payable, billing, inventory management, and such.
2. For professional firms like those of doctors, lawyers, and consultants:
   a. Time records: the number of hours each individual spent on each client or patient.
   b. Index of "know-how": a catalog of previous reports, assignments, cases.
   c. Client invoicing.
   d. Mailing list maintenance.
3. Mail-order firms:
   a. Order status reports. The status of every order is instantly available if a customer writes or phones.
   b. Customer billing.
   c. Mailing lists.
4. Utilities:
   a. Customer billing.
5. Process manufacturers:
   a. Order processing.
   b. Process control.
   c. Purchasing procedures.
   d. Inventory control.

14

A Computer in Your Office

If you do not now have a computer and are considering the lease or purchase of one, the steps in making the decision are:

1. Determine your objectives in automating.
2. Determine the scope of the automation.
3. Consider using a service bureau, possibly as an interim step.
4. Compare available computers and software.

DETERMINING YOUR OBJECTIVES

Rarely, in a small business, will a computer replace an employee. You do not automate to reduce the size of your staff, although you can relieve employees of some routine paperwork and create more time for important and profit-producing functions.

Your first step is to determine exactly what you hope to accomplish by automating. If you have several objectives in mind, list them in the order of their importance. Possible objectives are:

1. To handle specified office functions (accounts payable, accounts receivable, payroll, inventory, etc.) with greater accuracy.
2. To handle these functions with greater speed.
3. To reduce the amount of staff time spent on programmable routine procedures. The computer, if chosen wisely, should pay for itself in 2 years.

4. To be able to expand the administrative load with a minimum expansion in personnel.
5. To improve reporting techniques. The computer can print out just the exceptions that need human attention, rather than a complete list of data that must be studied to discover problems. For example, instead of printing all accounts receivable, the computer can be asked to print only those that are 2 months overdue.
6. To provide the instant availability of accurate and timely information, with an error rate of less than one-thousandth of 1%.
7. To make it possible to access more information, much more rapidly, than can be done with any manual or microfilm system. For example, J.C. Penney files in its computer all the relevant information about all its employees. When there is an opening, the "specifications" for the position are entered into the computer, which quickly prints a list of all the employees qualified for the position.
8. To provide one central file that can be accessed by terminals at remote locations.
9. To provide greater interchangeability of information between systems.

In considering automation, certain problems or disadvantages must also be weighed. Among them are the following:

1. Some technical skills are required to create computer programs that are not available ready-made, or even to modify ready-made software. Someone in the company can learn to program, a consultant or freelance programmer can be used, or if the volume of work justifies it a full-time programmer can be hired.
2. Automation can cause a total revision in the way of doing business. Some people are upset by the loss of manually maintained files.
3. There are security problems. Dishonest employees have been able to pilfer information from the computer or even cause it to write checks to nonexistent persons, which are then cashed illegally. A whole new industry specializing in computer security is springing up. Computer owners must take security precautions. Company executives have been held personally liable for failing to protect company data.
4. Maintenance of the stored tapes or disks can be a problem. They can be destroyed by fire, or by magnetic fields, or injured by dust or moisture. Tape heads must be cleaned periodically, and tape tension adjusted. Tapes consist of a mylar base holding tiny dots of iron that can be magnetized or not, just as a hole in a punch card can be open

or closed. Inaccuracy results if the tape is wound either too tightly or too loosely.

5. Duplicate "security copies" of important files must be maintained. The IRS has established "Vital Records Protection Procedures," which must be followed.
6. Start-up time almost invariably takes much longer than estimated. Lay out a very conservative time table—then double it!

For most small businesses the advantages greatly outweigh the disadvantages.

"SCOPING" YOUR REQUIREMENTS

The size and cost of the computer you will need are determined by the quantity of the data to be processed and the speed of processing and printing you need. In big companies this requires a detailed feasibility study, but you can fairly easily make a "vest-pocket" study to guide you in the selection of a computer.

For each function you are thinking of automating, answer these questions:

1. Word processing:
   a. Number and length of documents that must be stored
   b. Nature and frequency of changes made in master documents
   c. Number of pages of documents to be printed per day
   d. Quality of printout required
   e. Special requirements such as automatic addressing from a mailing list, insertions in the middle of the text, etc.
2. Accounts receivable:
   a. Number of customers
   b. Number of invoices per month
   c. Average and maximum number of lines per invoice
   d. Lead time—how fast are statements needed?
3. Accounts payable:
   a. Average number of accounts payable per month
   b. Total number of suppliers
   c. Number of individual items per statement
   d. Number of banks used
4. Inventory control:
   a. Number of items stocked
   b. Average and maximum number of transactions per month
   c. Speed and frequency of reports required
   d. Reorder frequency

5. Order entry:
    a. Average and maximum number of orders received per month
    b. Average and maximum number of items per order
    c. Order-handling procedure
    d. Types, frequency, and speed of reports needed
6. General ledger:
    a. Average and maximum number of entries per month
7. Special applications:
    a. Financial statements
    b. Analysis of return on investment
    c. Tax returns

An ingenious checklist that will give you a rough idea as to how badly you need a computer is given in Figure 14-1. It was prepared by Brian Callery, Product Manager, Philips Business Systems, Inc., and is reprinted by courtesy of *Modern Office Procedures* magazine.

ALTERNATIVES: SERVICE BUREAUS AND TIME SHARING

There are two possibilities to look into before you commit yourself to the purchase or lease of a computer: service bureaus and time-shared computer services.

Before looking at computer hardware or software, take your vest-pocket feasibility study to a service bureau—especially if you can find one that specializes in your industry or your type of business. See how much of the proposed automation the bureau can take over and how much it would cost.

There are many ways in which a small business can use a service bureau. For example, Iron Mountain Storage of New York used a bureau to handle the payroll for 60 employees for about $500 a month, saving about 10 hours of staff time and providing greater speed, accuracy, and access to records. Salmon Associates, consulting engineers, had a file of some 30,000 engineering reports they had completed. For less than $1,000 they stored the reports in a computer data bank, classified as to the industry, products, processes involved, and so on. Now they can instantly retrieve relevant information reports when they start a new assignment.

One advantage of working with a service bureau is that you can get into automation "piecemeal"—first one application and then another.

A service bureau may be the most economical way of handling some or all of the functions you wish to automate. Even if you eventually acquire a computer, the use of a service bureau can be a valuable interim

Test your company's computer needs

SALES/RECEIVABLES

1. Do you have more than 100 active accounts? ________
2. Do you have more than 50 active accounts with two or more ship-to locations? ________
3. Do you send out monthly statements? ________
4. If you send out monthly statements, do you send to all accounts? ________
5. Do you assess finance charges? ________
6. If you assess finance charges, do you assess all accounts? ________
7. Do you have established credit limits for each customer? ________
8. If you have credit limits, are these limits applied before an order is filled? ________
9. Does your business receive orders from at least two of the following sources: phone, outside salesmen, mail, other? ________
10. Do you employ more than five salesmen, whose remuneration is composed in part or whole of commission payments? ________
11. If answer to #10 is YES, are so-called "split commissions" ever paid? ________
12. Do you "age" your receivables? ________

INVOICING

13. Is your daily average more than 150 separate lines of billing? ________
14. Do you have peak periods throughout the year involving daily production of more than 250 separate lines of billing? ________
15. Do you average three or more lines of billing per invoice? ________
16. Are at least half of your invoices charge invoices? ________
17. Do you extend cost and gross profit on each invoice? ________
18. Do you provide trade discounts for at least some items at differing quantity and or price points? ________
19. Are cash receipts handled with formal documentation? ________
20. Do you currently prepare an analysis of sales? ________
21. Do you currently prepare reports on profitability by product and or customer? ________
22. If answers to #20 and 21 are NO, would such reports be helpful to your business? ________

PRICING POLICIES

23. Does your business offer selective pricing by customer? ________
24. Does your business offer quantity price breaks, e.g. per hundred, per thousand, per dozen, etc.? ________
25. Do you sell in fractional quantities or decimal quantities? ________
26. Is a conversion factor sometimes required to calculate prices? ________
27. Do you have no-charge invoices? ________
28. Is the line extension sometimes listed (lot price) as opposed to calculated? ________
29. Do you have freight-only invoices, or freight-to-follow situations? ________
30. Are 10 percent or more of your total orders back-oriented? ________
31. Are you required to collect taxes? ________
32. If answer to #31 is YES, do you collect taxes for more than two jurisdictions? ________

Figure 14-1

Checklist for Determining Practicality of a Computer (Reprinted from the September, 1978 issue of *Modern Office Procedures* and copyrighted, 1978 by Penton/IPC a subsidiary of Pittway Corporation.)

INVENTORY

33. Do you have more than 250 items in inventory? ________
34. Does your inventory turn at least three times a year? ________
35. Does your inventory include raw materials, as well as finished goods? ________
36. Does your business occasionally offer direct shipments from your vendor to the customer? ________
37. Are customer orders for standard (stocked) items handled separately from orders for non-standard items? ________
38. Is your inventory controlled in fractional units? ________

PAYABLES/CASH DISBURSEMENTS

39. Do you have more than 100 vendors? ________
40. Do you average at least 200 vendor invoices each month? ________
41. Do you average at least two distributions per invoice? ________
42. Does your business write more than 200 checks each month? ________
43. Are checks written on more than one account? ________

PAYROLL

44. Is there a time lag between pay period ending date and pay date? ________
45. Does your payroll include two or more of these standard pay periods: daily, weekly, bi-weekly, semi-monthly, monthly? ________
46. Are some of your employees paid on an hourly basis? ________
47. Are some of your employees paid on a salaried basis? ________
48. Are some of your employees paid on a commission basis? ________
49. Are hourly employees paid a differing rate for overtime? ________
50. Are salaried employees sometimes eligible for overtime payment at an hourly rate? ________

First the typical disclaimer: There are always exceptions, and it is conceivable that even though you answered 40 or more questions YES, your company still does not need a small computer business system. On the other hand, it is equally conceivable that even though you only answered 10 questions YES, it is time to get rid of the old posting machine and bring on a modern system. But, all exceptions duly recognized, here is the way we would evaluate the number of YES answers:

More than 40. Call a reputable small business computer manufacturer and pray that you can get a small computer system delivered tomorrow. Your need is critical. Be forewarned, though, that your prayer for overnight delivery will not be answered. Ninety days is the industry average from sign-up to start-up.

Thirty to 40. You have an objective need for a small business computer system, particularly if your company is growing at a rate in excess of the current inflation rate. But take your time, look around, call a number of manufacturers.

Twenty to 30. You are right on the line. Maybe you need a system, and maybe you don't. Experts would have to probe your particular situation in much greater detail.

Less than 20. Resign yourself to living with your faithful bookkeeper for another couple of years.

Figure 14-1 continued

operation in getting your procedures sufficiently well organized to be handled by a computer.

The other possibility is a time-shared computer service. Here the company offering the service has the computer and the computer program. You have a terminal in your office that is connected by telephone to their computer. You type in the data and get back the reports.

COMPARING AVAILABLE COMPUTERS AND SOFTWARE

If it appears that it would be practical for you to buy or lease a computer, do not be in too big a hurry! Shop around. Go to two or three possible suppliers in each of these categories:

1. Manufacturers, or dealers representing specific manufacturers, such as Radio Shack
2. Computer "stores," handling the hardware and software of several computer manufacturers
3. Computer consulting firms, which can make a more detailed analysis of your needs and recommend specific hardware and software

Your vest-pocket feasibility list will enable them to advise you on the size of computer you need and on the types and cost of software required.

As a very general preview of the costs you may be incurring, computers can be classified as follows:

1. Small microcomputers, for home or small business use. They have internal memories of up to 16K and can do basic calculations and data processing. They cost from $600 to $1,000, but this is just for the computer with its CRT. Add about $1,000 for the simplest printer if hard copies are required.

2. Larger microcomputers, with memories up to 32K, used by many small businesses. They cost from $2,000 to $5,000, plus $1,000 to $2,000 for a printer, depending upon speed and print quality required.

3. Minicomputers, with capacities up to 64K. They can perform all the functions a larger computer can, subject to limitations imposed by their slower speed. They cost from $5,000 to $25,000. (See Figure 14-2.)

Figure 14-2
A Minicomputer. This is the CADO Model 20/28, which can serve as the data processor, word processor, and message processor for eight satellite stations. (*Courtesy Dateline Communications.*)

4. Small business computers can handle all the functions required by most small to medium-sized companies. They cost from $25,000 to $35,000.

Selection of the computer will be influenced by the software available with it. This is discussed in the next chapter.

DETERMINING THE FEASIBILITY OF A COMPUTER APPLICATION

One question you may face, whether you are considering the purchase of a computer or already own one, is whether it would be feasible to use the computer for a particular procedure. There are eight factors involved in determining whether some process should be automated. If only two or three of these factors are involved, it is probably more efficient to handle the process manually.

The factors are as follows:

1. There should be a large volume of data involved.
2. The rapidity of producing the output is important.
3. The process is repetitive and can be standardized.
4. Accuracy or validity of the output is important.
5. There is considerable mathematical processing or data manipulation.
6. Multiple reports in various formats are required from the same basic data.
7. The application is a by-product of something the computer is already handling.
8. The automation will pay for itself in a fairly short time. As a general rule, it is not feasible to automate a procedure unless the automation will pay for itself in 2 years or less.

If the answer to a majority of these questions is "yes," the procedure should be automated. Table 14-1 shows how this feasibility test might apply to five possible procedures.

MAKING A FEASIBILITY STUDY

The "eight factors" list is a quick check of whether an application might be feasible. If it appears that it might be, you will want to make a more

Table 14-1
The Feasibility Test in Use

	Payroll	*Order Processing*	*Monthly Labor Summary*	*Long-Range Planning*	*Yearly Tax Report*
1. Large volume	✓	✓			
2. Speed required		✓			
3. Repetitive process	✓	✓	✓		
4. Accuracy important	?	✓			
5. Much calculation	✓	✓	✓		
6. Various reports needed *	✓	✓			
7. By-product of existing EDP			✓		✓
8. Rapid payback	✓		✓	N/A	

* Such as paychecks, payroll register, Social Security records, etc.

detailed feasibility study. The study and the conversion to automation include the following steps:

1. Systems Analysis

A good way to get a detailed picture of the entire procedure is to put yourself in the role of a document going through the system. What happens to you, where?

As you trace the procedure, ask yourself these questions:

1. Would it pay us to put this application on a computer?
2. What is wrong with our present method?
3. What is it that we cannot do at present?
4. What problems or complaints result from our present system?
5. What volume of documents is involved? What is the historical trend line in this volume? What has been the annual percentage increase in recent years?
6. How much staff time is required.
7. What are the processing requirements? What operations must be performed on the data?
8. What is the output now? What will be needed in the future?

2. Detailed Definition

1. Output requirements. Interview each person who uses the data. What information do you need? In what form: charts, tables, graphs, reports, exceptions? How often? How fast?

2. Input requirements. What information must be fed into the computer to get the desired reports? What do we have to do to get it? How much of it is presently available and how much represents additional input? What will it cost us to collect it?

3. Procedural Development

Using tables and flowcharts, develop the procedure for collecting the information, processing it, and formatting and distributing the reports. You face this situation:

Manually collected
data is available
↓
This gap is
filled in with
a program
↓
Data is processed,
formatted, and
distributed

4. Programming, Including Testing and Debugging

5. Implementation

1. Starting up new system
2. Period of parallel operation
3. New system takes over

15

Software Selection

Whether you are deciding which computer to buy or already have a computer and are planning to put some new application on it, a key problem is the selection and installation of the necessary software.

For most companies the investment in software is greater than the investment in the computer itself. Although the owners of some small businesses have written their own programs for their micro- or minicomputers, it is far more common for the business to buy ready-made or "commercial" software.

There are three reasons why it is usually more desirable to purchase a program than to develop one's own:

1. It is usually much less expensive. Costs of developing in-house programs are often much greater than anticipated.
2. It is almost always much faster to acquire a "shelf" program than to develop one's own.
3. The commercial program usually comes with more complete documentation.

Selecting the appropriate software package for a specific need is not easy. A recent issue of Computer World magazine estimated that there are more than 5,000 packaged programs on the market, ranging from Radio Shack programs costing $10 or so up to very sophisticated packages in the $100,000 range.

How does one make the software selection? This chapter outlines the major steps.

ESTABLISH A SYSTEMS EVALUATION TEAM

Put together a team consisting of both the people who will be using the program and the people who know something about data processing. This team will formulate the requirements and evaluate the available packages.

DEFINE THE SYSTEM REQUIREMENTS

Exactly what must the projected program accomplish? The "users" on your evaluating committee must answer these questions:

1. What is the problem to be solved?
2. In what environment will the system operate?
3. What input must be provided?
4. What outputs are needed?
5. How will this system interface with other systems?

And the "computer experts" on your committee will answer these questions:

1. What calculations will be required?
2. What volume of data must be handled?
3. What are the capabilities and limitations of the equipment?
4. What will the program language be?
5. How will the program interface with other software?

DETERMINE WHAT SOFTWARE PROGRAMS ARE AVAILABLE

Obtain lists and descriptions of possible programs from a number of sources, including:

- Data Pro Research Corp., 1805 Underwood Blvd, Delran, NJ
- Trade publications
- Software dealers
- User groups
- Management consulting firms in this field

SCREEN OUT PACKAGES THAT ARE NOT SATISFACTORY

There will be obvious reasons for eliminating some of the available packages, such as: the program is too new and untested; it requires a computer of a larger capacity than yours; it is written in a computer language you cannot, or do not wish to, use.

MAKE A DETAILED EVALUATION AND COMPARISON OF THE REMAINING PACKAGES

Questions to be asked about each possible program are:

1. Will the package meet our needs?
2. Will it run on our computer system?
3. How flexible is the package?
4. How difficult is it to install and use?
5. How many other users are there?
6. Is adequate documentation provided?
7. What support does the vendor provide?
8. What are the direct and indirect costs of the package?
9. What financial arrangements are offered?

ANALYZE THE VENDOR'S CAPABILITY, FINANCIAL STABILITY, AND PAST PERFORMANCE

Questions to be asked here are:

1. How long has the vendor been in the software business?
2. Is the vendor financially sound?
3. Does the vendor have a research and development program that will enhance the package after we have purchased it?
4. What sort of warranty is there?
5. Does the vendor offer an annual maintenance contract available after the expiration of the warranty period?
6. Does the maintenance agreement entitle us to remote support for a full year?
7. Does the maintenance agreement assure us of receiving all updates and enhancements?

8. What is the annual cost of the maintenance agreement?
9. What kinds of users are there?
10. Are these users likely to contribute to the enhancement of the program?
11. Who are the users in our industry?
12. Does the vendor provide a formal implementation guide?
13. Does the guide provide for two-way communications between us and the vendor?
14. How long does it take to implement the system?
15. How many man-days of support does the vendor provide?

CHECK OTHER USERS FOR THEIR EXPERIENCE WITH THE SOFTWARE

Most vendors will give you the names of other companies in your industry that are using their systems. Drop from consideration a vendor who will not or cannot do this; something is amiss. The vendor either is misrepresenting the users or knows that the users will tell you they are unhappy with the system.

Bear in mind the fact that unhappy users are unlikely to come right out and say, "We made a bad decision in purchasing this program." But if you ask, "What modifications would you recommend in the program?" you will probably smoke out any existing problems.

Another good source of user reactions is the "User Ratings of Proprietary Software" published by Data Pro. It is updated periodically.

NARROW YOUR SELECTION TO TWO OR THREE

It is unlikely that any one program will meet all your requirements, so weigh the value of the possible "trade-offs." One program may cost less than another but be more difficult to install. The program that seems to fit your needs most closely may come with less vendor assistance. Weigh these kinds of pros and cons in selecting the two or three that come closest to meeting your requirements.

SUBMIT DETAILED "APPLICATION QUESTIONS" TO THESE VENDORS

Based on your committee's specifications as to what is needed, ask each prospective vendor how the program will meet them. As an example, here is a list of the kinds of questions you would ask in selecting a program to handle general ledger and financial reporting:

1. How many positions can be used in the Account Number?
2. May the Account Number contain letters as well as numbers?
3. Can the Account Number be structured to meet my needs without my having to revise my existing Account Numbers?
4. May I encode memo information in unused positions of the Account Number, to be carried with the transactions for subsequent use in account analyses, without impacting the Master File?
5. Does the vendor provide a preprocessor capable of generating source code tailored to my hardware, software, and accounting environment?
6. If I change my hardware, software, or accounting environment, will I be able to modify the system to meet the new requirements?
7. May I enter both actual and budget data via journal vouchers?
8. May I enter statistical data via journal vouchers?
9. May I specify the effective date of each item on a journal voucher?
10. May I enter prior period adjustments via journal vouchers?
11. May prior period adjustments cross fiscal boundaries?
12. Does the system automatically adjust all the appropriate fields when prior period adjustments are entered?
13. May I enter future period transactions via journal vouchers?
14. Once set up, will the system automatically generate standard recurring entries each period without requiring any input instructions to do so?
15. May I enter accruals via journal vouchers?
16. Will the system automatically reverse prior period accrual entries each period?
17. May I mix actual, budget, financial, statistical, standard, accrual, prior period, current period, and future period transactions in a single batch?

SELECT THE SOFTWARE PACKAGE YOU WILL ACQUIRE

After reviewing this detailed information about your two or three "finalists," select the one that most closely fits your requirements, or can be modified to fit your requirements most closely, at the lowest total cost.

NEGOTIATE THE CONTRACT FOR THE SOFTWARE ACQUISITION

The contract should cover:

- Term of agreement
- Title
- Use of products
- Maintenance and support
- Warranty
- Nondisclosure
- Taxes
- Payment terms

INSTALL THE SOFTWARE

The vendor will normally consider its role in the installation to be complete when the promised documentation and training have been delivered and the package is running on your computer. However, the vendor should be responsible for its satisfactory operation until it has operated without problems for one processing cycle and has been fully integrated into your overall operational environment.

MONITOR THE OPERATION AND UPGRADE AS REQUIRED

Use the statement of requirements developed by your evaluation committee as a yardstick for making sure that the program is performing as expected. Adequate training of both existing and new personnel is important.

Modifying the program to meet your changing requirements is important in getting the maximum payoff from the system. Although the vendor may be coming up with various improvements and enhancements as part of the service package, use your own in-house expertise to constantly upgrade the system.

Selection of the "best" software package for a given application is a complicated task. There are many unknowns, many variables, and many "half facts" to deal with. But if you approach the selection systematically, you will be successful far more often than not.

16 Word Processors

A word processor (Figure 16-1) might be described as "a typewriter with a memory." It has a built-in computer, or is connected to a computer, so that a document can be typed, corrected, printed out, stored, and then printed later in its original form or with alterations.

Usually, the word processor has a CRT so the typist can see the text as it is composed on the keyboard. It is simple to edit this text as it is typed. Misspellings can be corrected; words, lines, or even paragraphs can be inserted or deleted; and the word processor automatically keeps the lines and paragraphs in order.

Regardless of how the original document is typed into the word processor, when it is printed out the "format" can be specific as desired—single or double spaced, wide or narrow margins, right margin justified or entire document set flush right, single or double spacing between paragraphs, indented paragraphs or flush left format, some material centered or in tabular form, and so on. The text can be printed out on single sheets of paper (in which case pages can be numbered automatically), on a continuous roll, or on forms such as address labels.

Word processors are of great value when some sort of standardized document must be typed, with or without modifications. A home improvement contractor, for example, might have a standard contract for installing new siding on a house. Most of it is standard text; all that needs to be changed are details like the specifications of the siding, color, completion date, cost, and payment terms.

The word processor types the document four or five times faster than a manual typist can, and without errors (assuming that the text has

Figure 16-1
A Word Processor. This is a dual display unit—there is a full-page, 66-line CRT and, in addition, the one line being typed is displayed in larger size just above the keyboard. The remote printer is at the left and disk drive at the right. (*Courtesy of Dictaphone Corporation, Rye, New York*)

been accurately copyread before being stored in the memory). Further, the document does not have the appearance of being mimeographed or duplicated; it is an individually typed letter, although not hand-typed.

An identical letter can be written to a number of individuals. If, for example, a distributor is taking several dealers on a cruise as winners of a sales contest, the typist has a form letter to go to the winners.

The typist inserts a sheet of stationery and types the address and first name (although even this can be done automatically on the more elaborate models): "Mr. Tom Jones, such-and-such address. Dear Tom:" The typist then presses a key and the form letter starts. "Congratulations on winning a cruise for you and your wife. We're glad to have you along. The ship sails from Pier X in Port City at noon on August 1. Your stateroom is No." The typing halts; the typist manually types in the number of Mr. Jones's stateroom and presses a key to continue the form letter.

It is easy to insert the recipient's name right in the middle of a paragraph. The last paragraph in the cruise letter might say, "And finally," The word processor stops; the typist inserts "Tom"; the form letter continues, "congratulations . . ." In the typed letter this appears as: "And, finally, Tom, congratulations on your outstanding performance last year. See you on the cruise!"

The ability to insert variations in an otherwise standard text makes word processors ideal for such applications as:

- Proposals
- Contracts and agreements
- Statistical and financial reports
- Product or structural specifications
- Engineering reports updated at intervals
- Directories of all types
- Policies and procedures manuals
- Technical and instruction manuals
- Newsletters
- Parts lists
- Mailing lists (most word processors can address labels or envelopes)

In addition to standard texts that are used again and again, "once only" texts can be done more efficiently on a word processor.

Consider an important business letter. It is a one-of-a-kind situation, so no standard form letter will suffice. With manual methods the author dictates a draft or types a rough draft. A typist types the final copy—and has to correct every mistake with correction paper or fluid, or by backspacing on typewriters with built-in corrections. The letter then goes to the author, who may decide to change something. Usually, the entire letter has to be retyped.

With a word processor, either the author or a typist types the letter into the memory, meanwhile watching it unfold on the screen. Corrections are made instantly. When the letter is finished, it is typed out without error at about 400 to 500 words per minute. If the author wishes to change something, the typist merely brings the letter back up onto the screen, makes the change electronically and retypes the letter in seconds.

Relatively new on the market are "electronic typewriters." These have a very limited memory—half a line or so—so the typist can make sure the words are correct before they are transferred to the paper. Electronic typewriters with larger memories are akin to word processors with very small memories.

Table 16-1
Decision Table: Manual Typing Versus Word Processor

1. Average number of pages of *programmable* material typed daily
2. Analysis of programmable material:

	Type of Document	*No. of Each per Day*	*Avrg. No. of Words in Each*	*Total Words*
a.				
b.				
c.				
d.				
	Total number of programmable words			

A. Staff Cost Using Manual (Electric) Typewriters

3. Total words per day ÷ 45 words per minute = minutes spent daily typing programmable materials ______
4. Multiply line 3 by cost per employee minute to get cost per day of typing programmable materials ______
5. Multiply line 4 by 264 (number of *days* per year the average office is open) to get annual *staff* cost of typing programmable materials ______

B. Staff Cost Using Word Processors

6. Total words per day ÷ 150 words per minute (allowing for preparing initial text, individual inserts, etc.) = minutes spent per day typing the same materials ______
7. Multiply line 6 by cost per employee minute to get cost per day of typing material on word processor ______
8. Multiply line 7 by 264 days per year to get annual cost of staff time with word processor ______

C. Cost Comparison: Lease, Buy or Do Without a Word Processor

	Do Without (includes cost of electric typewriter)	*Lease*	*Buy*
1. Annual staff cost (from lines 5 and 8)			
2. Annual "owning" cost:			
(a) Total cost ÷ years amortized		xxx	
(b) Annual interest on half the cost		xxx	
3. Lease cost	xxx		xxx
4. Annual cost of service contract		(included)	
Totals:			

Table 16-2
Sample Decision Table: Manual Typing Versus Word Processor

1. Average number of pages of *programmable* material typed daily
2. Analysis of programmable material:

Type of Document	*No. of Each per Day*	*Avrg. No. of Words in Each*	*Total Words*
a. Proposals	2	1000	2000
b. Replies to price requests	4	500	2000
c. Sales letters	10	250	2500
d. Status reports	5	500	2500
Total number of programmable words			9000

A. Staff Cost Using Manual (Electric) Typewriters

3. Total words per day ÷ 45 words per minute = minutes spent daily typing programmable materials — 200
4. Multiply line 3 by cost per employee minute to get cost per day of typing programmable materials — $30.00
5. Multiply line 4 by 264 (number of *days* per year the average office is open) to get annual *staff* cost of typing programmable materials — $7,920.00

B. Staff Cost Using Word Processors

6. Total words per day ÷ 150 words per minute (allowing for preparing initial text, individual inserts, etc.) = minutes spent per day typing the same materials — 60
7. Multiply line 6 by cost per employee minute to get cost per day of typing material on word processor — $9.00
8. Multiply line 7 by 264 days per year to get annual cost of staff time with word processor — $2,376.00

C. Cost Comparison: Lease, Buy or Do Without a Word Processor

	Do Without (includes cost of electric typewriter)	*Lease*	*Buy*
1. Annual staff cost (from lines 5 and 8)	$7,920	$2,376	$2,376
2. Annual "owning" cost:			
(a) Total cost ÷ years amortized	250	XXX	2500
(b) Annual interest on half the cost	75	XXX	750
3. Lease cost	XXX	$3,000	XXX
4. Annual cost of service contract	75	(included)	200
Totals:	$8,320	$5,376	$5,826

Note: The "owning" cost of the electric typewriter assumes a $750 cost written off in 3 years = $250 per year and interest at 20% on half of $750 = $75. Similarly, the "owning" cost of the word processor is $7,500 written off in 3 years = $2,500 per year plus interest at 20% on $3,500 = $750.

In considering whether your office should have a word processor (or another word processor, if you already have one) you first define what basic kind of processor you need. There are two types:

1. You can buy a typewriter with an internal memory of about 40 pages. An example is the Qyx "Intelligent Typewriter," which retails for about $2,000.
2. If you need to store longer documents or a greater variety of documents, you will need a processor with an external memory on mag cards, tapes, or disks. Here again you face two choices:
   a. You can buy a word processor designed primarily as a word processor. These cost $12,000 to $15,000, can print rapidly in a variety of typefaces, and in general are highly versatile machines.
   b. You can buy a word processing program for a microcomputer like the Radio Shack TRS-80 or the Apple. The computer, program, and printer cost $4,000 to $5,000. The advantage here is that you have a full-fledged computer, capable of handling other office functions. As word processors, however, the computer hybrids are not as efficient as the "purebred" word processors, some of which can also be programmed to perform simple arithmetic functions like billing.

For larger offices, several word processor keyboards can be connected to a central memory unit. In this application it is advisable to have one or two "freestanding" word processors so that the whole department is not shut down if something goes wrong with the central unit.

Can you afford a word processor? Table 16-1 is a "decision table" you can use in determining whether a word processor would be economically justified in terms of staff time saved. Table 16-2 is a filled-out example.

17
Copiers and Duplicators

The term "copier" or "office copier" will be used to refer to a device that prints from one to 20 copies directly from an original document. A "duplicator" is a device for reproducing hundreds of copies, not from the document itself but from some kind of plate.

Some offices have both kinds: a copier for making two or three copies of documents when required and a duplicator for direct mail letters, newsletters, and the like.

SELECTION OF A COPIER

Basically, there are two types of copiers: "plain paper" copiers, which can make a copy on any piece of paper, including your own letterhead or forms; and "coated paper" copiers, which make copies only on a special paper.

If you compare two copiers with approximately equal speeds, the coated stock copier will usually be considerably less expensive. If all you need are legible copies of documents to read, they are adequate. The plain paper copiers, on the other hand, produce a much clearer copy, with greater contrast between the text and the paper. It is easy to write on the copy and to erase this writing—actions that are almost impossible on the coated paper copiers.

The other principal variable that affects the price of a copier is its speed. If your office is going to be making only two or three copies an hour, you can get by with one of the slowest ones. If you will be reproducing as many as 100 pages a day, you will need a copier capable of turning out at least 10 to 15 copies per minute.

Once the basic choices as to type of paper and speed are made, here are some other considerations:

What Are the Copy Requirements?

1. What types of documents will you be reproducing?
2. Will you need to reproduce pencil originals? Black-and-white photos? Color photos?
3. What size documents will you have to copy: nothing larger than "letter size" (8½ × 11″), or "legal size" (8½ × 14″), or larger engineering drawings?

What Quality of Reproduction Is Desired?

Do you really need "perfect" copies? The office copier is used ideally as a substitute for another typing operation; the copies usually go into a file where they are referenced infrequently. If you can use a copier that can merely produce clear, legible copies rather than "perfect" ones, you will save a lot of money.

Who Will Use the Equipment?

If everybody in the office will be cranking out copies, select a copier that is simple to operate and has a minimum number of controls. If only one or two "experts" will be using the copier, you can select one that is more complicated to operate if it provides other benefits.

How Permanent Must the Copies Be?

Some copiers produce relatively short-lived copies, which fade when exposed to light and are too thin to stand up under frequent handling. Will this serve your purpose, or do you need copies that will last longer and withstand handling?

Will the Copies Be Written on?

Some types of copies are difficult to write on with a pencil, and writing on them is impossible to erase. Should this be a factor in your selection?

What Are the Costs per Copy?

You naturally consider the costs of chemicals, special paper, or other supplies needed. But these are just part of the true costs per copy. Also consider:

1. Waste. If the process will result in some number of unsatisfactory and discarded copies, add the supplies cost of these.
2. Reproduction time. If it is slow, add the cost of the additional staff time.
3. Travel time. If the copier must be located in some remote place, how many minutes of staff time will be lost in going to and from the location (with allowances for stops at the water cooler and friendly conversations en route)?
4. Waiting time. Will one person have to wait while another person is running copies? If so, add this to staff time.

Will the Copier Function in Your Work Location?

When you have narrowed your choice to two or three copiers, arrange for a trial period of each copier in your office. The copier that worked so well in the showroom may be less efficient in your office because of light levels, voltage variations, or the difficulty experienced by your employees in using it.

THE "LEASE OR BUY" DECISION

There are three ways to acquire a copier:

1. Purchase it. In this case, you can sign an annual service contract with the supplier or simply pay for service as required. If you can get a good service arrangement with a local dealer, it is often more economical to buy a used copier.
2. Lease it. In this case you pay so much per month, plus so much per copy. Service is usually included.
3. Rent it. This costs more per month but does not tie you up to a longer-term lease.

The method of deciding whether to buy, lease, or do without a copier is described in Chapter 12. This decision depends upon the cost of the machine and the number of copies to be made on it. As a general

Figure 17-1
Quick Reference Chart Selection of the "Best" Method for Reproducing or Duplicating Copies

Type Duplication or Reproduction Process	Electrostatic Transfer	Electrofax (Direct Electrostatic)	Offset Duplicators	Spirit Duplicators	Stencil Duplicators
Partial Brand/Model Listing	Xerox 8131 Xerox 914 Xerox 2400	Apeco Dial-A-Copy Bruning Copytron Dennison Copier A.B. Dick 650	Multigraphics, A-M Royal Zenith Hamadastar 7700X	Heyer Spirit, 3M	A.B. Dick Mimeo Gestetner 3M Speed-o-Print Heyer Mimeo
Number of Copies Economically Produced	1 to 15	1 to 15	Short-run mat: 15-200 Medium-run mat: 200-700 Long-run mat: 750-2500 Metal: 2000 +	15-200	15 to 2000 copies
CHARACTERISTICS OF ORIGINAL DOCUMENT					
Types of Copy That Can Be Reproduced By This Process	All legible originals (drawing, printed matter, charts) printed on one or both sides	All legible originals (drawing, printed matter, charts, printed on one or both sides)	Any legible material (including photos) reproduced on coated paper or metal master plates.	Material typed, handwritten or drawn, etc., on special masters	Any material typed, handwritten, drawn or facsimile reproduced on special master
One or Two Sided Printing	Either	Either	Either as desired	One	Two if facsimile reproduced, otherwise one

Size Limitation	Up to 11″ x 17″	Up to 11″ x 17″	Up to 17″ x 24″	Up to 8½″ x 14″	Up to 8½″ x 14″
Quality Required	Legible	Legible	Legible	Legible	Legible
CHARACTERISTICS OF REPRODUCED COPY					
Size Limitation	Reproduces same size as original (size reduction is an option)	Reproduces same size as original	Up to 16″ x 23½″ maximum	Up to 8½″ x 13½″ maximum	Up to 8½″ x 13½″ maximum
Copy Quality	Equal to original	Equal to original	Equal to original	Fair (less than original)	Fair to equal to original
One or Two Sided Printing	Usually one	Usually one	Either as desired	One	Either as desired
Type and Surface of Paper	Uses either standard weight paper or special translucent coated paper	Uses coated paper in either sheet or roll format	Uses offset bond of 16# or higher: card stock, etc.	Uses special duplicator or 20# weight .	Uses mimeo bond of 16# or higher weight
Estimated Life	Equal to original	Equal to original	Equal to original	Equal to original if not continually exposed to light	Equal to original

rule, if you make more than 3,000 copies a month, it will be cheaper to buy the copier than to rent it. This same chart can be used to compare two competitive models.

DUPLICATORS

The two most commonly used types of duplicators are:

1. Those using a "direct image" plate. This is a treated paper master; you write, type, or draw directly on it, it is mounted on a multilith press, and each plate will produce 100 to 200 copies. You can make changes on the plate by scraping off the existing copy and writing or typing the new copy.

2. Those using a photographic plate, which can reproduce an unlimited number of copies. The original copy is photographed onto a film negative, which is used to prepare a metal offset plate. This is actually a form of offset printing.

Mimeographs, hectographs, and other equipment employing typewritten stencils are less widely used today.

In making more than 15 copies, the simplest and cheapest procedure is to make a direct image plate on a Xerox copier and use that as the master on a multilith. It costs less to make and run the master on a multilith than to run copies on the Xerox at 3¢ to 5¢ each.

A chart comparing the various types of copiers and duplicators is shown in Figure 17-1.

18

Microfilm and Microfiche

"Microphotography" or "micrography" is the general term for the photographing of documents down to a greatly reduced size. It helps reduce storage space—the contents of a three-drawer file cabinet can be photographed onto a roll of film about the size of a typewriter ribbon—but is somewhat inconvenient to access.

Herewith the answers to some common questions about the microfilming of files:

WHAT ABOUT LEGALITY?

Under the Federal "Uniform Photographic Copies of Business Records in Evidence Act" of 1951, microfilm copies of business records can be used as evidence in federal courts and legal procedures. A "Certificate of Authenticity" is photographed as the last document on the reel.

All states except Louisiana and the Commonwealth of Puerto Rico have enacted legislation affirming the legality of microfilm records. Even in these states, judges have ruled, under a concept known as the "best evidence rule," that microfilm records can be introduced in evidence if the originals no longer exist.

On the other hand, various federal and state regulatory agencies have differing rules about the maintenance of microfilm records instead of paper documents. For example, the IRS and the SEC permit financial files to be maintained on microfilm, provided that a duplicate back-up copy is maintained in some other location. The Civil Aeronautics

Board (soon to disappear) requires that some documents be maintained in their original paper form for 2 years; after that they can be microfilmed and the originals destroyed. Wisconsin does not permit microfilming for trust records. New York State has minimum quality standards that the microfilm copies must meet.

As a rule, unless you are in a heavily regulated industry like insurance, securities, or utilities, you need have no fear that there are any regulations barring the use of microfilm, so long as you comply with the generally accepted quality control and image standards, accuracy of indexing, and security protection.

WHAT FORMATS DOES MICROPHOTOGRAPHY USE?

The microfilm copies can be made either from documents or directly from a computer memory by means of "COM"—Computer Output Microfilming.

The available formats are:

1. Nonunitized, in which the documents are photographed continuously onto a roll, cartridge, or cassette of microfilm. All sorts of documents can be jumbled together on the reel. This format is the best for minimizing storage space, but the worst for retrieval.

2. Microjacket, a card approximately 5 × 8″ into which three strips of microfilm can be inserted. Each card can carry some kind of alphabetical or numeric designation, which helps in retrieval. Material can be added or updated by changing one of the strips.

3. Microfiche, a piece of film approximately 3 × 5″ on which 225 pages of 8½ × 11″ documents can be reproduced. Columns are numbered and rows are lettered, so that a particular page of a document can be located in the index as, for example, "Fiche No. 86, C-6."

WHAT ABOUT COSTS?

A study made in 1980 indicated that the cost of transferring quantities of 8½ × 11″ documents onto ordinary microfilm was about 2¢ per exposure or 1.5¢ per page when in-house, slightly more when done by a microfilming service bureau.

In projecting your costs, allow for the cost of storage. Microfilm will last for 100 years but must be stored at 35% to 50% humidity and 60 to 72 degrees Fahrenheit. When storage costs are included, it is usually less expensive to store documents in their original paper form unless they must be kept for more than 8 years.

HOW IS THE INFORMATION RETRIEVED?

This is where microfilm is inconvenient. The rolls or fiche of film must be indexed in some way. The desired roll is then fed into a reader, or the microfiche is placed on the reader's projection tray. The reader itself is bulky and not portable. It projects an enlarged image of the document on a glass plate that looks something like a CRT.

Documents are usually filmed as negative—white text on a black background—which some find difficult and tiresome to read, although the screen is similar to that of a word processor. If filmed in positive form—black on white—there is considerable glare from the white portion of the document.

A reader costs from $200 up; one that can also print paper copies of retrieved documents costs about $2,000. Two desks can sometimes share one reader if it rotates on a lazy Susan.

WHAT ARE SOME TYPICAL APPLICATIONS?

Microfilming can be used to keep a record of orders. That data can go into microfilm directly from a computer, and can be indexed by customer's name, zip code, SIC number, or the like. Brokers use microfilm to maintain records of transactions or of securities going into or out of the vault.

Part Four

MORE EFFICIENT PEOPLE

19 Motivating Your Employees

A well-known story about motivation concerns the manufacturer of a consumer product who conducted a sweepstakes promotion. Purchasers of the product could send in a coupon that entered their names in a prize drawing. First prize was unique: The winner would be taken into a bank vault after business hours. There the winner would see a large mound of silver dollars, a shovel, and a wheelbarrow. The winner would be allowed to keep all the silver dollars he or she could shovel into the wheelbarrow and remove from the vault in a specified time period.

In setting up its budget for the promotion the company needed to estimate the cost of this first prize. So it sent one of its huskier young advertising executives to the bank and tried it out. He succeeded in getting $22,500 in coins out of the vault, so the sum of $25,000 was earmarked for first prize.

The young man who actually won the contest succeeded in getting $45,000 out of the vault in the same length of time! The first man was going through the motions; the second was motivated.

In seeking to improve office efficiency the manager can never lose sight of the fact that staff members who really *want* to turn out more work *can* turn out more work, without any change in equipment or procedures. Similarly, much of the potential efficiency of time-saving equipment is lost if it is used in a slipshod manner.

What are some of the factors that motivate employees? We will look first at some of the well-known theories about motivation, then offer our own suggestions.

THEORIES OF MOTIVATION

The "Hawthorne Principle"

Back in 1927 a group of Harvard Business School psychologists headed by Elton Mayo conducted an experiment in the Western Electric plant in Hawthorne, Illinois, near Chicago. They were interested in determining the effects of the environment upon worker productivity.

The group they studied consisted of a number of women who were winding small coils. Since they were paid on a piecework basis, they should theoretically have been motivated to turn out the largest possible number of parts. After measuring the normal rate of production, the researchers improved the lighting. Productivity went up. Then they added an extra recess period, with free hot chocolate. Productivity went up some more.

Then they took away the hot chocolate—but productivity continued to climb. They reduced the lighting to its former level, and productivity went still higher. They reduced it even further, and productivity climbed again.

The scientists concluded that these women were motivated, not so much by coffee breaks and lighting levels, but by the fact that somebody was paying special attention to them. They were important. They didn't know why these professors with white smocks and clipboards were concentrating on their department, but they were certainly receiving all kinds of attention.

In short, the manager helps to motivate an employee simply by taking an interest in that employee. Even a poor training program produces results if it makes the employees feel they are getting some kind of special treatment. This phenomenon has become known as "the Hawthorne effect."

In another study conducted at a plant of Johnson and Johnson, supervisors were shown a long list of factors that might affect employee morale and were asked to select the ten most important ones, ranking them in order of their importance. Employees who reported to these supervisors were shown the same list and asked to rank them in the order of their importance in building employee morale.

Strangely enough, the factor that rated at the bottom of the managers' list was Number 1 on the employees' list. It was simply this: "The boss listens to me. If I'm bothered by something, I can talk to him and he hears me, rather than just giving me the dust-off."

The way to motivate those who report to you, then, is to take an interest in them as individuals. How much do you really know about these employees? If you want to test yourself, use the form in Table 19-1. In the first column, list all the factors you feel that you as the

Table 19-1
How Well Do I Know My Employees?

	Names of Employees								
Bits of Information I Should Know About Each Employee									

manager should know about each employee—for instance, approximate age, marital status, age of children, birthday, hobbies, ambition, and so on. After completing the list, fill in the names of employees who report to you at the tops of the other columns. Then, in the column for each employee, put a check mark opposite the bits of information you do know. How many blank boxes in your complete chart?

The McGregor Principle

The late Douglas McGregor of MIT originated the idea that managers usually believe in either "Theory X" or "Theory Y." "Theory X" is the old-fashioned belief that people are inherently lazy, will shirk responsibility, and will perform their work only when threatened by a stick or enticed by a carrot.

If people behave that way, said McGregor, it is because we have been treating them that way since the beginning of the Industrial Revolution, and people tend to act the way they are expected to act.

He pointed out that the same individual who appeared so listless on the job was often a dynamo of activity after hours in hobbies, community activities, and sports. People really do want to work and accept responsibility, he said, if they understand the goals of the organization and of their role in it, and are given some responsibility. This is "Theory Y."

The Pygmalion Effect

Pygmalion, according to an ancient Greek legend, was a sculptor who carved an ivory statute of a beautiful woman, Galatea, and then fell in love with his own creation. The legend was the basis of a play by George Bernard Shaw and of the musical comedy, "My Fair Lady."

The Pygmalion effect in psychology refers to the fact that people tend to perform in accordance with their superior's expectations of them. Some actual examples:

- An elementary school teacher was told that two pupils, actually selected at random, were highly gifted and that two others picked at random were slow learners. Sure enough, some months later the two tagged as superior were leading the class and the two supposedly inferior learners were lagging.
- A group of insurance salesmen was divided into three groups based upon their sales accomplishments: superior, average, and inferior. They were assigned to different managers, who were told which group

had been assigned to them. A year later the superior performers were still leading the pack; the inferior performers had mostly failed. But the manager to whom the median group had been assigned was determined that the men were more capable than their records indicated. He worked with them in the expectation that they would succeed—and the percentage of sales increase for this middle group was greater than that of the superior group.

In short, your staff will tend to mirror your expectations of them.

Maslow's Hierarchy of Values

The late Abraham Maslow formulated the well-known theory that individuals have a hierarchy of needs and that each individual is motivated by the lowest unfilled need. This hierarchy is shown in Figure 19-1.

At the bottom are the most basic physical needs for food, clothing, and shelter. Until this level of need is filled, a person will strive only for these necessities of life and will not be motivated by any of the higher needs. A starving person will not be motivated by the offer of a merit badge or a testimonial letter.

Once the immediate physical needs are filled, the next drive is for security, for the assurance that the physical needs will continue to be filled. Someone who has plenty to eat will not exert extra effort for another sandwich but will work to save money or hang onto a job so that there will be food on the table tomorrow.

After present and future physical needs have been assured, an individual seeks love, in the broadest sense of the word. We want to be accepted by relatives and associates; we want to feel that we "belong." Ostracism by one's peers is almost insufferable.

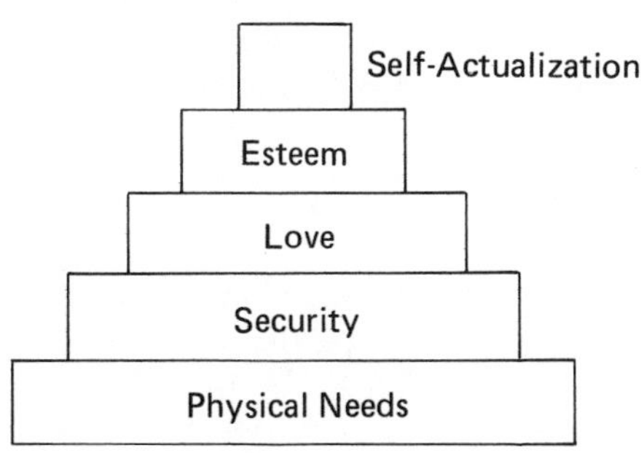

Figure 19-1
Maslow's Hierarchy of Needs

If this need is filled, the next higher need is recognition or esteem. We want the world to be aware of our accomplishments. We want our names to be known.

Finally, if all these are filled, the only remaining motivator is the drive for self-fulfillment, the awareness that we have made the best use of our talents, led a worthwhile life, left the world a bit better than it was before we came along.

You can observe this principle at work among your staff. For example, if they feel insecure about their jobs, they will concentrate on nailing down the present job or finding another one and will not be motivated by offers of recognition.

Job Enrichment

Most companies offer their employees medical insurance, paid vacations, a pension plan, and other fringe benefits. Are the employees more highly motivated as a result?

Frederick Herzberg of Pittsburgh analyzed the factors that made employees want to work harder or to shirk. He found that the usual fringe benefits did nothing to motivate employees. He called them "hygienic factors"—if the company does not offer them, the employee will leave for a company that does, but their existence does not inspire additional efforts.

What does motivate employees, he found, was an opportunity to develop their abilities, to have some say in how the job was to be done, to take more responsibility (not too different from McGregor's "Theory Y"). Herzberg developed the idea of "job enrichment": broadening the scope of a job to make it more challenging and less monotonous.

In a typical automobile plant, each worker performs one tedious task as an unending procession of cars moves past on an assembly line. The Volvo company in Sweden tried forming workers into teams and letting each team build the entire automobile. Workers were much more interested in their work, which now became meaningful and challenging.

Behavioral Psychology

B. F. Skinner, the "father" of behavioral psychology, was a pioneer in establishing the importance of "feedback"—letting the individual know, as quickly as possible, how well his or her performance measured up to expectations. Dr. Skinner believes that all our beliefs, habits, and behavior have been programmed into us because we received "positive feedback"—some type of psychological reward—when we did them.

He started his experiments with pigeons. He found he could teach them to dance a tango step by using the principle of positive feedback to "reinforce" the behavior pattern he was trying to create. Assuming that the tango step started by putting the right foot forward, Skinner waited until the pigeon accidentally put its right food forward and immediately rewarded it with a grain of corn. Before long, the pigeon would put its right foot forward as soon as it was put into the experimental cage.

If the desired sequence was "right foot forward, left foot sideways," Dr. Skinner then waited until the pigeon, after doing the first step correctly, accidentally did the second one in the desired manner. More reinforcement.

This is called "shaping behavior." By rewarding the behavior we want, we can shape the behavior of a pigeon—or a person, according to Dr. Skinner.

He was the originator of "programmed learning," in which the student applies one bit of knowledge and immediately gets positive feedback by learning that he or she answered the question correctly.

The application of this principle to office management is that the manager lets everybody know, as soon as possible, "how they're doing."

Ed Feeney, a consultant in behavioral psychology, applied this principle while he was employed by Emery Air Freight. His suggestion cost Emery not a cent, was put into effect overnight, and increased the company's profits by nearly a quarter of a million dollars.

The situation was this: Emery Air Freight collects individual packages from hundreds of shippers and accumulates them at loading docks all over the country. The packages are then delivered to the appropriate airlines to take them to their destinations. At each loading dock there are bins or igloos, each one labeled for packages destined to the same city via the same airline flight, like "American Airlines 106 to Dallas." If packages are placed in these preconsigned bins, rather than being delivered individually, Emery gets a lower freight rate. But it was easier for employees to toss the individual packages into a pile marked "Texas."

Employees at the docks, as well as their supervisors, said that about 80% of all packages for which a bin was available were actually put into the correct bins. Actually, despite frequent instructions and pleas by Emery, the figure was closer to 20%.

Mr. Feeney applied Skinner's principle of immediate feedback. On each loading dock was posted a large checkoff chart. Every time an employee put a package in one of the designated bins, he or she put a check mark on the chart. Everyone—the individual worker, the supervisors, any visitor—could see immediately what a good job this crew was doing of getting packages into the bins. Feedback was all it took.

Management by Objectives

Many psychologists have pointed out that workers perform better when they have a clear idea of the objectives of their job, and some influence in determining those objectives.

In the managerial technique known as "Management by Objectives," or "MBO," the top executive of the organization sets the objectives of the organization in consultation with immediate subordinates. Then each subordinate sets the objective for his or her department in the same way; the people under them in turn set their objectives; and so on down the line. These objectives should be concrete, measurable achievements, so that the task of each manager is simply to help each employee who is falling behind on an objective.

Management Styles

The attitude and motivation of workers are obviously affected by the character and behavior of their manager. Managerial styles range from autocratic and dictatorial at one extreme, through various degrees of participative management, to a sheer do-nothing attitude at the other extreme.

David L. McClelland, a psychologist at Harvard University, has studied what he calls the achievement motive. Some people are driven by the desire to achieve, quite apart from any profit or recognition that may result. A strong achievement motivation in managers, however, influences them to try to do everything themselves, rather than develop the abilities of the employees. In a good manager, McClelland finds, the desire for power is stronger than the desire for personal achievement. This does not mean dictatorial power, but simply an urge to influence others to perform in a way that is best for the company. See "Power is the Great Motivator," by David C. McClelland and David H. Burnham, *Harvard Business Review*, March-April 1976.)

THE SIX QUESTIONS

Based on our own experience as consultants working with scores of companies, the authors suggest that there are six basic questions you must answer if your staff is to be motivated and efficient. These questions can never be completely answered; a good manager is consistently providing more complete answers to them. The questions are as follows.

1. What Is the Job? What Am I Supposed to Do?

This may sound obvious, yet the manager and the subordinates rarely view the subordinate's job in exactly the same light. The Human Relations Institute at the University of Michigan asked a number of managers, "What are the four most important tasks performed by the employees who report to you?" Then they went to the employees and asked, "What are the four most important tasks your boss expects of you?" There was only a 30% correlation between the job as viewed by the boss and the same job as viewed by the employee. If work is to be done efficiently, there must be close agreement as to what the job is.

The standard answer to this question is a job description, specifying the functions the employee is expected to perform. Yet even this is not a perfect answer, for when several people are doing the same thing, there are individual variations in performance based on experience, temperament, intelligence, and other factors. The job description is really the basis for a discussion between manager and employee about what is to be done, why it must be done, and the relative importance or priority of the various aspects of the job.

2. How Am I Supposed to Do It?

The answer to this question, of course, is training. The effective manager knows what knowledge and what skills are required for the performance of the subordinates' jobs. The manager provides this knowledge and these skills by some combination of the three basic avenues of training. They are:

- *On-the-job-training,* in which the manager or a trainer first shows the employee how to do something, then watches the employee do it and—following Skinner—reinforces what the employee did correctly and corrects what the employee did incorrectly.
- *Group training,* such as classroom instruction or seminars, which may be conducted by the manager personally, by some other department of the company, or even by an outside organization.
- *Self-instruction,* such as correspondence courses, textbooks, cassette tape programs, or even computer-assisted instruction.

3. How Well Am I Supposed to Do It?

What is par for the course? How well am I expected to perform all those tasks listed in my job description? How many letters am I expected to write in an hour, how many telephone inquiries, how many claims?

The answers to that question can be called performance standards, targets, objectives, or any other name; the important thing is that the employee has a clear, specific idea of what constitutes acceptable performance. These are minimums; the standards set the floor. The extent to which the employee may exceed them is a matter of motivation.

4. How Am I Doing, and
5. What Should I Be Doing Differently?

"How well am I doing? What does the boss think of my work? How do I stand in this company?"

There is a deep-set human desire to know the answers to such questions, yet many companies do not supply them. The manager feels embarrassed to sit down privately with an employee and discuss the employee's work.

Some companies have initiated formal programs of "evaluation and counseling," often with disappointing results. Too often the manager is asked to evaluate the employee on psychological traits, such as "initiative" and "cooperation." How do you measure initiative? And how do you enhance it in an employee deemed deficient in it?

A quarterly or semiannual performance review can be very constructive, however, if it is based on an objective and measurable set of performance expectations. It is comparatively easy for the manager to compliment the employee on those parts of the job done well and to work out ways of improving performance where it has fallen short. This subject is discussed in more detail in Chapter 25.

6. What's in It for Me if I Do?

This is the question of motivation. Answers to the first five of these six questions go a long way toward motivating employees. McClelland's studies referred to above indicated that employee morale was high when the job was well organized and good performance was recognized.

Financial motivation must be considered. Employees do work harder if there are bonuses based on individual performance or on total office accomplishments, or some type of profit-sharing plan. Money itself is usually not a motivator, but it is a symbol of the other motivators in Maslow's pyramid; it provides security, it indicates recognition by the company, it provides comfort for one's family, and it adds to the esteem in which the wage earner is held.

In addition, there are a number of different drives, which vary greatly from individual to individual, and it is up to the manager to find out which drives are strong and which are weak in each of the individuals reporting to him or her. Among these drives are:

1. Recognition
2. Fair treatment
3. Performing socially significant work
4. Opportunity for advancement

5. Competitiveness—the desire to do better than somebody else
6. Respect for one's boss and one's company
7. The feeling of teamwork or "togetherness"
8. The feeling that "my company keeps me informed—I need not fear unpleasant surprises"
9. The desire to be liked by others

If a manager is aware of each individual's psychological needs, the manager can see to it that the employee gets more of what he or she wants by giving the company more of what it wants.

20
Compensation and Fringe Benefits

How much should you pay each employee? How do you determine what raises to give them? Should you have some kind of incentive compensation plan or profit-sharing plan? These are some of the questions we will tackle in this chapter.

BASE SALARIES

There is a "going rate" in your community for each type of office worker. If you offer less than the going rate, you will not be able to recruit new employees, and some of your present staff may leave. (Possible exception: If people have a high job satisfaction, they may stay with a small firm for less money than they could earn somewhere else.) If you offer too much more than the going rate, you increase your costs unnecessarily and make it difficult to meet competition.

You can get a feel for this going rate by noting the salaries offered in help wanted ads, talking with other office managers in similar occupations, and discussing salary requirements with employment agencies when you are seeking a new employee.

It is difficult for older executives to make the mental adjustments for inflation. If the salary demanded by a beginner seems twice what it should be, remember that the dollar is worth only half what it was 10 years ago.

Once the employee is on the payroll, you face the problem of the annual raise. There are two kinds of raises:

1. A "cost of living adjustment," often abbreviated to COLA, which simply corrects for the declining purchasing power of the dollar. If living costs go up 10%, the employee needs a 10% raise just to maintain his or her existing standard of living. The COLA adjustment enables the employee to keep on paying for the present apartment, but not to move into a better one.

This is a relatively recent phenomenon, which helps keep the inflationary pot boiling. Raises formerly were given only for increases in productivity, and many small office managers still react negatively to the idea of a COLA.

2. Merit increases, which should be in addition to COLA increases, represent an increase in the employee's real income because of increased experience, productivity, and value to the organization.

If an employee's contribution is worth 10% more this year than last and if the rate of inflation has been 10%, that employee merits a 20% raise—10% to keep up with the cost of living and 10% more because of greater productivity or value.

Most managers agree that it is better for employee morale if raises are given voluntarily by the company without the employee's having to ask for them.

If the company has a regularly scheduled performance review, is this the time to announce the increase in salary? Opinion is divided. Some feel that the salary announcement should not be made at the same time as the performance review lest that be the only thing the employee remembers about the interview. Others feel that it is logical, almost inevitable, to couple a review of the employee's productivity with an announcement of the corresponding change in base salary.

Some small business managers give each employee an annual statement showing the cost of the fringe benefits paid for on behalf of that employee. Staff members usually do not realize how much the owner pays for Social Security, workmen's compensation insurance, health programs, and pension programs. This knowledge may make the employee's expectations about the size of the pay raise a bit more modest.

PENSION PLANS

Anything one may say about company pension plans must be tempered by the fact that in the late 1970's, federal regulations made it so expensive to administer corporate pension plans that many companies dropped them altogether. Attempts are currently under way to simplify government regulations, so pension plans may again be worth considering.

There are two principal reasons for inaugurating a pension plan:

1. From the humanitarian standpoint, it is a lot easier to let a faithful employee retire at 65 if the manager knows that the employee will not be totally dependent upon Social Security.
2. From a business standpoint, the existence of a pension plan helps to retain valuable employees.

A pension plan can be either contributory, meaning that the employees chip in a portion of the cost, or noncontributory, meaning that the company pays it all. When the employee retires, he or she pays income tax on that portion of the pension contributed by the company. The company can administer its own pension fund or deposit the payments with an insurance company.

One type of pension plan is a "profit-sharing plan." Here the company deposits into the pension fund some specified portion of its profits each year. The contribution will of course be larger in more profitable years, and it can be zero in a losing year.

If your company does not have a pension plan and is thinking of inaugurating one, talk with two or three pension plan consultants as well as with two or three insurance companies.

INCENTIVE COMPENSATION

If the rationale of the base salary is "a day's work for a day's pay," the rationale of the incentive compensation plan is "a little something extra in your paycheck for an outstanding day's work."

The manager says inwardly—not to the staff!—"If I can boost profits 20% more than they would be otherwise, I'll be willing to give the staff (often including the manager) one fourth of that extra profit." This incentive compensation plan would add about $3 in additional profits for every $1 paid out in bonuses.

The simplest of all incentive plans is just to let the employees know that some percentage of all the profit, or a larger percentage of the profit over some target figure, will be distributed as bonuses.

Theoretically, it is not fair to base the employees' bonuses on net profit, since for tax reasons the manager may deliberately hold down the net profit. However, where there is mutual trust between employees and boss, it is a simple plan. And it does not mean that the manager must give employees confidential information. If they want to share in the bonus plan, they take the manager's word for the size of the melon.

Ingenuity can be exercised in developing the formula that determines the individual employee's share of the bonus pool. For example:

1. The size of the bonus can be based strictly on the employee's salary. Everybody gets 2 weeks' pay, or 4 weeks' pay, or whatever the profit amounts to. An employee making $25,000 a year will get twice as big a bonus as one making $12,500. This is fair enough, since the base salaries reflect each person's value to the company, so the bonus is being distributed in proportion to value. There are two ways to calculate this type of bonus:
   a. Add up the weekly base salaries. Divide this total into the total bonus dollars. The result is the number of weeks' salary each person will receive as a bonus.
   b. List all the weekly or monthly salaries and total them. Divide this total into each individual's salary to determine that person's percentage of total salaries. Each individual then gets his or her percentage of the bonus pool.
2. The bonus can be weighted for longevity, thus rewarding those who have stayed with the firm longest and making it increasingly difficult for them to leave for another job. In effect, you increase the bonuses of those who have been there longest by taking something away from the bonuses of the newer employees, thereby keeping the bonus total constant.

   One possible way to apply this method is to determine that each person's bonus will be increased 1% for each full year of employment—or 2% or 3% or whatever you wish, depending upon how much importance you place on longevity. You can, if you wish, place a "cap" on this formula; for example, the bonus will be increased 2% of each year of employment up to a total of 40% (or whatever top you select).

   You determine the basic bonus on the basis of salary, as explained above. The total of these bonuses will equal your predetermined bonus pool. Now increase each person's bonus by the percentage earned for longevity. Add up these adjusted bonuses; the total will of course be greater then your bonus pool. Divide this larger adjusted total into the original bonus pool; you will get a decimal fraction smaller than 1. Multiply each individual's adjusted bonus by this fraction to get the new bonuses weighted for longevity.
3. If you have some way of measuring individual productivity, you can increase the bonus for the more productive employees by working out a productivity formula similar to the longevity formula.

It is suggested that the bonus be based on some kind of mathematical formula as in the examples given above, rather than on the manager's subjective judgment as to each employee's "loyalty," "initiative," or other ill-defined and unmeasurable characteristics. Subjective evaluations can produce misunderstandings and disagreements.

How frequently should the bonus be paid? In general, the more frequent the payments, the greater their motivating value—unless the individual sums become too small to be impressive.

A quarterly payoff period works for most companies. If you fear that you might pay out a share of profit in the first three quarters and then show a loss in the fourth quarter, pay out only some fraction of the calculated bonus—half or three fourths—in the first three quarters, then make the final bonus payment on the basis of the total year's results.

21

Employee Relations and Federal Regulations

It is important for the office manager to be familiar with government regulations such as the wage-hour law and the various laws against discrimination. A manager may honestly feel, "I'm a fair-minded person and don't discriminate against anybody"—and yet innocently and unintentionally take some action resulting in a charge, an investigation, and the loss of a great deal of time, legal fees, and possibly fines.

This chapter will review the two areas of regulation that can cause trouble for the small office: wage-hour laws and antidiscrimination laws.

WAGE-HOUR LAWS: WHO IS COVERED?

A great many small offices come under the wage-hour regulations of the Fair Labor Standards Act (FLSA) even if they are not engaged strictly in interstate commerce. "Covered" businesses include:

1. Any enterprise doing a gross volume of business of $250,000 or more
2. Enterprises having workers engaged in interstate commerce, producing goods for interstate commerce, or handling materials that have been moved in or produced for interstate commerce
3. Retail stores or chains of stores having annual sales of $362,500 or more
4. Laundries and dry cleaners
5. Construction or reconstruction companies

6. Hospitals; homes for the sick, aged, or mentally defective; and pre-school, elementary, secondary, or higher schools—all covered whether operated for profit or not

Even if an office does not fall under one of these "covered" categories, individual employees are covered by the act if they are:

1. Communication and transportation workers
2. Employees who handle, ship, or receive goods moving in interstate commerce
3. Clerical or other workers who regularly use the mails, telephone, or telegraph for interstate communication or who keep records of interstate transactions
4. Employees who regularly cross state lines in the course of their work
5. Employees of independent contractors who perform clerical, custodial, maintenance, or other work for firms engaged in commerce or in the production of goods for commerce

(Although the following comment takes us outside the domain of the office, it should be noted that domestic service workers such as maids, day workers, housekeepers, chauffeurs, cooks, and full-time baby-sitters are covered if they receive at least $50 in a calendar quarter and work a total of more than 8 hours a week for one or more employers.)

If your company is not covered by the Fair Labor Standards Act, you probably are subject to your state's laws, which usually are quite similar to the federal laws. We will summarize the federal laws; if they do not apply to you, write to the appropriate body in your state to check the state laws. For a summary of the U.S. law, write to the U.S. Department of Labor, Employment Standards Administration, Wage and Hour Division, 200 Constitution Avenue, Washington, D.C., 20210 and ask for a copy of the booklet "Handy Reference Guide to the Fair Labor Standards Act," WH Publication 1282.

OVERTIME PROVISIONS

The main thing to remember about the wage-hour law is: Employees must be paid at the time-and-a-half overtime rate for any time worked more than 40 hours a week.

Even if the employee volunteers to work an additional hour for nothing, the manager must pay for the overtime. Further, if the employee does the overtime work voluntarily, without the manager's knowledge, the manager is still responsible for paying for the overtime. The manager, in short, cannot *permit* employees to work overtime unless they are paid time-and-a-half.

The only exception is that when the employee has worked overtime, the employer may elect to give the same amount of time off out of future hours. If so, this compensatory time off must be taken within the same "work week."

The work week is any 7-day period you wish to use. It can, for example, run from Monday to Monday, or from Wednesday to Wednesday. If your work week runs from Monday to Monday and somebody works overtime Friday evening or Saturday, you must pay them overtime rates—there is no more working time left in your work week. But if your work week runs from, say, Thursday to Thursday, if somebody works Saturday you can give them Monday or Tuesday off in compensation (if they prefer that to the money) because it is still in the same work week.

MINIMUM WAGES AND CHILD LABOR

The FLSA establishes a minimum wage of $3.35 an hour. Under certain circumstances, learners and apprentices can work for less than that, or even for free. Check with your State Department of Labor if you would like to use trainees.

The act also regulates child labor. If you employ teenagers, full or part time, be careful to comply with the act. For example, 15-year-olds cannot work after 7 P.M. in the winter or 9 P.M. from June 1 to Labor Day.

The safest rule is: When in doubt, check with your lawyer.

Managers of small offices often feel, "We're just one happy family. The staff doesn't mind working a little bit late now and then to catch up on the paperwork." But the "one happy family" picture disappears when one disgruntled employee quits and files a claim for back pay. Investigators come into your office and question other members of your staff.

"Do you have to work a little longer some evenings to catch up?"

"Oh, sure, now and then, but we're glad to do it. Our manager is such a nice person."

"Does the manager pay you for the overtime?"

"Oh, no, we wouldn't think of asking for pay for chipping in to do our share."

Wham! Now the manager is subject to back pay claims, possible fines, all kinds of trouble.

Do not let your people work overtime unless you pay them the overtime rate!

Sometimes there are after-hours activities such as a cocktail party given by one of your suppliers, a trade show, or some kind of meeting. If the manager so much as suggests that it would be a good idea for the employees to attend, they must be paid overtime. The only way to avoid the overtime payment is to tell the staff, orally and *in writing*, that attendance at the event is purely voluntary and that failure to attend will not in any way reflect undesirably on the employee.

ANTIDISCRIMINATION LAWS

Violation of the laws against discrimination, however unintentional, can be very costly. The successful complainant may win hiring or reinstatement, promotion, transfer, and back pay. The court usually orders a losing employer to pay all legal fees and court costs.

Where courts find discrimination against groups of women or minorities, the settlement can be steep; for example, $2 million by Chase Manhattan, $32 million by General Electric, $75 million by AT&T. In addition, the court often dictates the terms of future employee activity relating to the disputed jobs, so that management loses much of its decision-making authority.

Basically, you cannot deny anyone an equal opportunity for employment or advancement because of that person's "race, color, religion, sex, or national origin." There can be no encumbrances, artificially created and unrelated to the work, to hinder a person from performing a job he or she can do.

The Regulations

The federal regulations are as follows.

Equal Pay Act (1963)

This act prohibits pay differentials on the basis of sex. A woman must be paid as much as a man if she is doing a job that requires equal skill, responsibility, effort, and working conditions.

Title II of Civil Rights Act (1964)

This prohibits discrimination in employment practices on the basis of race, color, religion, sex, or national origin. "Employment practices" include all conditions that affect employment, such as selection, wages, training, promotion, discipline, and termination.

Executive Order No. 11246 and Revised Order No. 4 (1965)

This order applies to government contractors. While the Civil Rights Acts specifies what an employer must *not* do, this executive order tells a government contractor or subcontractor what he or she *must* do. It requires a contractor to take affirmative action to increase the number of women and minorities in the organization, to establish an internal auditing system to measure the effectiveness of its program, and to agree to let the Department of Labor inspect its personnel files on any matters relating to these subjects. This latter provision has imposed problems and costs on many companies.

Age Discrimination in Employment Act (1967, amended 1978)

This act makes it illegal, in all employment practices, to discriminate on the basis of age against any individual between 40 and 70.

Rehabilitation Act (1973)

This act bans discrimination against qualified handicapped individuals in hiring, placement, advancement, or any other employment process or employee benefits. A government contractor is required to take affirmative action to recruit and train handicapped individuals who are qualified to handle the job.

Veteran's Readjustment Act (1974)

This act requires employers to take affirmative action in employing and advancing disabled veterans and veterans of the Vietnam era.

Enforcement Procedures

The Equal Employment Opportunity Commission (EEOC) is a five-member federal commission that enforces the Equal Pay Act, Title VII of the Civil Rights Act, and the Age Discrimination Act. It has jurisdiction over companies that have more than 15 employees and are engaged in interstate business. It cooperates with state antidiscrimination agencies.

The Office of Federal Contract Compliance Programs (usually abbreviated to OFCCP) administers Executive Order 11246, the Rehabilitation Act, and the Veteran's Readjustment Act. Firms handling contracts or subcontracts with the U.S. government should familiarize themselves with the details of these three laws. Since the equal opportunity laws apply to all employers, only they will be discussed a bit more fully here.

The EEOC distinguishes two types of discrimination:

1. *Overt* discrimination is the specific, unequal treatment of an individual because of sex, race, color, religion, or national origin. *Example:* Company A hires women to do packing jobs because they are "better at sit-down work that requires manual dexterity." Men are hired as stock clerks because of the lifting and moving of materials. This practice denies women the opportunity of securing a stock clerk's job solely on the basis of sex (assuming they are capable of doing the moving and lifting). If experience as a stock clerk is important in getting promotions, this practice makes it more difficult for women to win promotions.

2. *Systemic* discrimination is the result of a policy that is, on the surface, fair and neutral but actually affects a larger proportion of one group than another. *Example:* Company B requires its stock clerks to be 5′8″ or over, feeling that such persons are better able to reach materials stored in awkward places. However, since the proportion of males over 5′8″ is much higher than the proportion of females of that height, this policy results in the hiring of many more men than women. *Another example:* The Duke Power Co. required all employees to have a high school diploma, without regard to race, color, or sex. This seemed to be fair and was applied equally to all applicants. The problem was that in its area a much higher percentage of white persons had completed high school than black persons and a high school diploma was not really necessary for many of the jobs, so this practice was ruled to be systemic discrimination.

There are four basic gauges you can apply to all personnel decisions —including hiring, performance appraisal, promotions, rewards, and terminations. Your decisions will not violate EEOC rules if they are:

1. Job-Related

Consider only those factors that relate specifically to the performance of the job. We cannot assume that a characteristic or ability *may* affect the employee's work; we must demonstrate a concrete relationship.

2. Objective

Use only specific, measurable data that is free from your own values, feelings, and prejudices. Factors such as attitude, aggressiveness, maturity, initiative, and intelligence are not valid criteria. See Chapter 24 for a discussion of productivity measurements.

3. Consistent

Decisions used in selecting, evaluating, and promoting employees must be applied equally to all candidates and employees.

4. Without Adverse Impact

Even if your criteria are objective and consistent, they cannot have an adverse impact upon women or minorities; there can be no systemic discrimination. Your practices cannot screen out a disproportionate number of women or minorities. If you are using a criterion that does have an adverse affect, such as a height requirement, the government requires you to prove that it is an actual necessity.

In determining whether a policy has an adverse effect, the EEOC uses the "four-fifths" rule. The percentage of women or minority applicants hired must be at least four fifths of the percentage of male majority applicants hired.

For example, you interview 20 white males and hire eight of them. You have hired 40% of the applicants. Four fifths of 40% is 32%. That means you must hire 32% of the women or minorities you interview. If you interview 12 women, your hiring policies will be considered to have an adverse effect unless you hire at least four of them ($12 \times 0.32 = 3.84$). The basic procedure of the EEOC or a state agency is as follows:

1. A charge is filed on behalf of an individual or a group of individuals.

2. The agency notifies the company and begins to gather information by examining documents and interviewing individuals. There can be a negotiated settlement at this point.

3. The agency may find there was not "reasonable cause" for the charge and dismiss it. If the agency finds reasonable cause to believe the charge is true, it tries to settle by conciliation.

4. If conciliation fails, either the commission or the individual may sue. In fact, the individual can sue even if the commission did not find a reasonable cause. The EEOC may file a systemic charge against a company, if its policies appear to be neutral and applied equally to all classes but ultimately result in a denial of equal opportunity to minorities or women.

Employment Procedures

A basic guideline is: When hiring a new staff member, think about the job that has to be done, not about the kind of person you want.

In interviewing applicants, ask about the job and how the applicant might handle it, not about the applicant. Specifically, do not ask questions about the applicant's:

- Religion
- Home ownership
- Family
- Marital status
- Age

If you advertise to fill a job, the EEOC requires you to keep copies of the ad for 1 year.

As you interview applicants, keep careful notes of each individual's qualifications for the position and keep the notes in your files as evidence that your final selection met the four gauges cited above.

Keep objective records on all employees (not just minorities), and make sure that promotions as well as terminations are based on the four valid gauges.

The equal opportunity laws are not just a nuisance. As one experienced personnel executive states, "Don't consider EEOC as just a big bad wolf. You may actually do a better job of selecting employees if you base your decisions on objective criteria."

And Tim O'Sullivan, Deputy Director, Administration, of the New York Zoological Garden, which has nearly 1,000 full-time and part-time employees, adds, "At no time does the law demand that you take incompetent people and put them in jobs where competency is demanded."

SEXUAL HARASSMENT

Sexual harassment is prohibited under both the Civil Rights Act and Executive Order 11246; current guidelines on the subject were published by the EEOC in October 1980. Sexual harassment is defined as unwelcome sexual advances, requests for sexual favors, or other physical or verbal abuse. Laws against it apply to both supervisory and nonsupervisory personnel.

The EEOC has established three criteria for determining what behavior is illegal:

1. Submission or rejection is an explicit or implicit condition of employment.
2. Submission or rejection is used as a basis for employment decisions.

3. The conduct unreasonably interferes with an individual's work performance or creates an intimidating, hostile, or offensive work environment.

The responsibilities of the employer are:

1. To do everything possible to prevent sexual harassment by:
   a. developing and distributing to all employees a policy against it,
   b. letting supervisors know that disciplinary action will be taken if any misconduct is found, and
   c. incuding the topic in affirmative action seminars.
2. To let employees know whom to go to with a complaint.
3. To take immediate action to correct the situation if a complaint is filed.

OTHER REGULATIONS

Other federal regulations are beyond the scope of this manual. Among them are:

- OSHA (Occupational Safety and Health Act), designed to protect employees from dangerous or harmful factors in the work environment.
- FICA (Federal Insurance Contributions Act), which regulates IRS and Social Security deductions and payments.
- ERISA (Employees Retirement Income Security Act), which regulates company pension plans.

OSHA investigators have the right to show up at any time, without preliminary announcements. Representatives of all the other agencies, however, must arrange to see the employer at a time convenient to the employer.

22
Recruiting and Selection

Haste and carelessness in recruiting new employees can produce a number of "white elephants"—staff members who are not bad enough to fire but not good enough to promote. Incompetent staff members greatly increase the burdens on the office manager. So let's take a look at the generally accepted methods of recruiting and selecting new staff members—nothing startlingly new, perhaps, but a useful review of the basics.

JOB DESCRIPTIONS AND "PEOPLE SPECS"

The recruiting process starts with two documents: a job description and a "person specification." If you do not have them, write them before starting the search for that new employee you need; if you do have them, review them to see if they need updating.

The job description simply tells what the employee is supposed to do. It may tell who the employee reports to or what the salary range is, but the most important part is a detailed listing of all the functions the employee will be expected to perform.

The "person spec" is the answer to the question: "What kind of person do I need to find to handle these chores?" Be sure to limit your statements to the minimum specific requirements needed to handle the job. Be careful not to let prejudices as to race, sex, age, or education affect your list of specifications.

For example, if the employee will be expected to deliver heavy packages by car, do not specify that a man will be needed; many women can drive cars and lift heavy packages, too. The spec should simply read: "Must have valid driver's license, be able to drive car, and to carry bundles weighing up to 40 pounds."

SOURCES OF RECRUITS

The most frequent mistake made in selecting new employees is the failure to interview enough applicants for the job. It stands to reason that if you interview 20 applicants you will have a much better chance of finding a satisfactory one than if you interview only five.

Where do you find these applicants?

1. Continuous recruiting. Always be on the lookout for "suspects." At parties, at church functions, at club meetings, while riding on trains, buses, or airplanes, be on the lookout for people who might be desirable staff members. You can explain, "We don't have an opening right now, but when there is one would you be interested in working for our company?" Keep a card file of these "suspects," and when there is an opening get in touch with them.

2. Employment agencies, whether private or government-operated. These can be helpful if you give them a copy of your job description and person specifications and insist that they send you only applicants who meet the qualifications.

3. Newspaper help wanted ads. Write an ad that makes the job sound interesting and challenging. State the qualifications clearly as a means of screening out unqualified applicants. You will usually get more applicants if you give a phone number to call, rather than requiring the applicant to write a letter to a box number. Most people find that they get a better response if they give the name of the firm; many people will not answer "blind" ads for fear that they might be applying to their own company. If you are located in the suburbs or outskirts of a city, be sure to use the nearby suburban papers. Many people who are not willing to commute downtown will apply for a job in their neighborhood.

4. Members of the present staff. Let them know when there is a job open and encourage them to send in any friends who may be qualified or to look for candidates. Some companies pay a bonus to the employee who suggests a successful job applicant.

5. Schools. Contact schools that train people in the kind of work you need done—salesmanship schools for sales personnel, secretarial schools for secretaries, programming schools for computer operator.

6. Clubs. Sales executives clubs, advertising clubs, and service clubs like Rotary and Kiwanis often have employment committees.

7. Trade associations.

8. Supplier salespeople may know of persons looking for your kind of job.

9. Customers are a possible source of suggestions.

Each time you hire someone, keep a record of the sources you used, the number of applicants received from each source, and the number eventually hired. This is called "validating" your sources; it will give you a clue as to where to concentrate your efforts.

THE SELECTION PROCESS

The usual steps in the selection process are these:

1. A brief preliminary interview, by phone or in person, to see if the candidate meets the basic qualifications.
2. An application blank, to be filled out by the candidate and carefully studied by the hirer in preparing for the depth interview.
3. A detailed interview, following up the information on the application blank. In some companies, two or more managers interview each applicant and compare notes.
4. A check of previous employers.

THE SCREENING INTERVIEW

This interview should be as brief as possible. The main purpose is to see if the candidate meets the minimum specifications. For example, the candidate may be required to type at a certain speed, or to take dictation, or to operate a keypunch machine.

To encourage applications, some companies make it easier for applicants by listing a phone number in the ad and asking them to phone, even on Sundays. If the preliminary interview is conducted by phone and the candidate seems qualified, the candidate is invited to come to the office to fill out an application blank. (If this would be quite inconvenient, the application blank can be mailed.)

THE APPLICATION BLANK

(Ready-made application blanks are available at major stationery stores if you company does not already have such a blank. A typical example is given in Figure 22-1.

Study each applicant's filled-out form carefuly, making notes of questions you will want to bring up in the depth interview. Things to look for in the application blank are:

1. General appearance. If the form is extremely messy, illegible, or incomplete or includes numerous strikeovers, you would hardly expect the candidate to be neat and methodical.

2. Unexplained gaps in the applicant's personal history, during schooling or employment. Sometimes these gaps are not easy to spot on the form; jot down the dates chronologically on a bit of scrap paper to see if there are any gaps. The reason for the gap may be a quite simple and innocent one, but you will want to go into it during the interview.

3. Many short-time jobs. If the person has been a "job jumper" in the last 5 or 10 years, the habit may well persist after the person joins your office.

4. Lack of progress in job history. You prefer an applicant with long tenure with previous employers, but if there was no advancement during this period it may indicate complacency or lack of drive.

5. Self-employed or in family business. Be careful of candidates who have recently operated their own business or worked in a family business—especially if the business has failed.

If you have been fortunate enough to attract a number of candidates, use the application forms to select the eight or ten that seem most promising.

THE DEPTH INTERVIEW

The following tips on conducting the interview are excerpted with permission from a home-study course on recruiting and selection produced by Porter Henry & Co., Inc., of New York City:

1. Follow the plan for the interview made while studying the application form.

application for employment

We are an equal opportunity employer, dedicated to a policy of non-discrimination in employment on any basis including race, creed, color, age, sex, religion or national origin.

PERSONAL INFORMATION Date ______ Social Security Number ______

Name ______ Last ______ First ______ Middle ______

Present Address ______ Street ______ City ______ State ______ Zip ______

Permanent Address ______ Street ______ City ______ State ______ Zip ______

Phone No. ______ Height ______ Weight ______

State Name and Department of Any Relatives, Other Than Spouse, Already Employed By This Company ______

Referred By ______

Last ______ First ______ Middle ______

EMPLOYMENT DESIRED

Position ______ Date You Can Start ______ Salary Desired ______

Are You Employed Now? ______ If So May We Inquire of Your Present Employer ______

Ever Applied to this Company Before? ______ Where ______ When ______

EDUCATION	Name and Location of School	Circle Last Year Completed	Did You Graduate?	Subjects Studied and Degree(s) Received
Grammar School			☐ Yes ☐ No	
High School		1 2 3 4	☐ Yes ☐ No	
College		1 2 3 4	☐ Yes ☐ No	
Trade, Business or Correspondence School		1 2 3 4	☐ Yes ☐ No	

Subjects of Special Study or Research Work ______

What Foreign Languages Do You Speak Fluently? ______

Read ______ Write ______

Activities Other Than Religious (Civic, Athletic, etc.) ______

EXCLUDE ORGANIZATIONS, THE NAME OR CHARACTER OF WHICH INDICATES THE RACE, CREED, COLOR OR NATIONAL ORIGIN OF ITS MEMBERS.

Form M660-26NR Printed in U.S.A.

(Continued on Other Side)

APPLICATION FOR EMPLOYMENT

Figure 22-1
Wilson Jones
Application For Employment
(Front) M660-26NR

FORMER EMPLOYERS List Below Last Four Employers, Starting With Last One First

Date Month and Year	Name and Address of Employer	Salary	Position	Reason for Leaving
From To				
From To				
From To				
From To				

REFERENCES: Give Below the Names of Three Persons Not Related To You, Whom You Have Known At Least One Year.

Name	Address	Business	Years Acquainted
1			
2			
3			

PHYSICAL RECORD: Do you have any physical condition which may limit your ability to perform the job applied for?

In Case of Emergency Notify
Name Address Phone No.

I authorize investigation of all statements contained in this application. I understand that misrepresentation or omission of facts called for is cause for dismissal. Further, I understand and agree that my employment is for no definite period and may, regardless of the date of payment of my wages and salary, be terminated at any time without any previous notice.

Date Signature

DO NOT WRITE BELOW THIS LINE

Interviewed By Date

REMARKS:

Neatness		Character	
Personality		Ability	

Hired For Dept. Position Will Report Salary Wages

Approved: 1. Employment Manager 2. Dept. Head 3. General Manager

Figure 22-1 (continued)
Wilson Jones
Application For Employment
(Back) M660-26NR

2. Put the candidate at ease. Suggest that he or she call you by your first name if that is appropriate.
3. Resolve to do more listening than talking.
4. Ask broadly worded, open-ended questions: not "Did you like the job?" but "Tell me something about the job." And after asking the question, *listen!*
5. Follow up on any information given by the applicant that is incomplete, negative, or unclear. Use questions such as, "In what way was it difficult?" or a "reflection" type question—"You found it difficult."
6. Maintain a permissive, receptive attitude throughout. Look interested, lean forward periodically, murmur agreement and understanding.
7. Compliment on favorable data and avoid any sign of disapproval toward unfavorable data.
8. When taking notes, be brief and businesslike, not furtive. If you want to note an unfavorable item, wait until you are on a new subject before writing it.
9. Bridge from one subject to another by commenting on the subject just covered and setting up the next. 'That must have been interesting helping to set up the new office. Tell me about your next job."
10. Do not ask leading questions that "give away" or "plant" the answer. Example of a leading question: "Neatness is very important in this office. Would you say you're a neat person?"
11. Speak naturally, athough if you tend to be a rapid talker, slow down a bit. The slower pace will contribute to the applicant's relaxation.
12. Smile often, react warmly, be friendly.

A good screening question is to describe some kind of problem that might arise on the job and ask the candidate, "How would you handle it?"

If you decide that the candidate is not suitable for the job, merely explain that you will be interviewing a large number of candidates and will get in touch with him or her as soon as you can. After the final selection has been made, write to the unsuccessful candidates explaining that you selected those best fitted to the job from a large list of applicants.

If you are favorably impressed, let the candidate know that he or she is in the running, spend a little time selling the applicant on the desirability of the job, and promise to get in touch. If the applicant is not selected, write that you selected the best from a large number of good candidates but are keeping his or her name on file for consideration when there is a future opening.

CHECKING PREVIOUS EMPLOYERS

This should be done by phone, or even in person if practical. Reason: If you write, the previous employer will be reluctant to put any unfavorable comments into writing.

Phone the employer, explain that so-and-so has applied for a position with your company, and say that you would appreciate some information.

Verify the applicant's statements about the position held and the salary earned.

Ask open-ended questions about the applicant's work, as well as about how he or she got along with the other employees, responded to supervision, and so on.

Ask if the employee had any habits or tendencies that would interfere with success in your company. If there is any hesitation, probe for the reasons.

A good final question is, "If so-and-so wanted to go back to work for your company, would you hire him (or her)?"

In addition to checking previous employers, check the applicant's educational accomplishments if that is important to the position. Do not take it for granted that the applicant has a master's degree in business administration just because he or she says so. For some reason, employers rarely check educational qualifications; applicants know it and frequently exaggerate their scholastic attainments.

23
Training

If an employee fails to perform some function adequately, the manager should ask himself or herself these five questions:

1. Does the employee *know* he or she is supposed to do the job?
2. Does the employee know *why* he or she is supposed to do it?
3. Does the employee know *how* to do it?
4. Does the employee know *how well* he or she is expected to do it?
5. Does the employee know why it is to his or her personal *benefit* to do it well?

Answers to most of these questions have been covered in earlier chapters. A good job description tells the employee what he or she is supposed to do; explanations by the manager explain the importance of each function. Performance standards or agreed-upon objectives tell the employee how well the job should be done. In appraisal interviews the manager can point out how the employee benefits by performing the job adequately—"positive reinforcement" in terms of incentive payments if they exist, a sense of achievement, better relationships with customers or other employees, job security.

In this chapter we will cover the answers to that third question: "*How* am I supposed to perform each of these functions?"

The answer is training: initial training for new employees and continuation or "refresher" training, if needed, for experienced employees.

Initial training is usually easiest. The new employee is eager to learn and willing to accept suggestions. Continuation training may be a bit more difficult, as experienced employees may find the training boring or adopt a know-it-all attitude.

INITIAL TRAINING

A policies and procedures manual and a job description are the two documents that help make initial training efficient. Without them you will be covering the same ground anyway, but in a more random and haphazard manner.

If more than one person is involved in training new employees, the training responsibilities, needless to say, must be specifically spelled out.

There are only three basic ways in which training can be provided:

1. Individual training, or "one-on-one" coaching. This is easily the most effective form of training, especially in skills.
2. Group or classroom training, either "in-house" or at some outside training organization. Large corporations that add new employees in groups often use classroom training at least initially.
3. Self-study training, such as books to read, or self-study courses in text or cassette form.

On-the-job coaching is the method usually used in small offices. If the job description is complete and up-to-date, it lists each function the employee will be expected to perform. The trainer can take them one at a time and go through the following steps:

1. Explain what the task is and why it is important.
2. Tell how it is done.
3. Show how it is done.
4. Have the new employee do it, and—
5. Compliment the newcomer on what has been done correctly and point out the correct way when there have been errors.

Repeat steps 4 and 5 until the employee is comfortable handling the task.

CONTINUATION TRAINING

As the first step in planning the continuing training program, the manager sits down once or twice a year with a list of employees and makes a note of the training each employee will need in the near future.

Periodic appraisal interviews are the best possible way of defining such training needs. In their absence, measurement of work output or simply observing the employee in action will also define needs.

Training requirements are not limited to employee deficiencies in present procedures. Often new equipment, such as a computer or word processor, or new procedures will require that perfectly capable employees receive specific training.

Since small offices cannot afford too many specialists, it often pays to train people to be "pinch hitters" in tasks they do not ordinarily handle—or at least let them know who else in the office has the know-how in these areas. Some night you may have to add paper to the copying machine after your secretary has gone home.

With a list of who needs what in the way of training, the manager then decides how, when, and where it is to be provided. Depending upon the subject matter, there are a number of possibilities:

1. On-the-job coaching by a knowledgeable person within the company.

2. In-house group training sessions. To maintain the interest and involvement of the more experienced employees, use a variety of training methods, including role playing if applicable. Above all, get group participation.

3. Outside training classes conducted by the supplier of the computer or software, or by associations like the American Management Association or your trade association.

4. Training sessions, individual or group, conducted on your premises by an outside expert. Companies that sell complicated computer software usually provide some training of this type.

5. A variety of self-study methods, ranging from ordinary correspondence courses to computer-assisted training.

Training employees in sales skills is a special subject beyond the scope of this book. If your employees are expected to do some selling, recommended books on salesmanship are:

- *Effective Selling Through Psychology* by V. R. Buzzota, R. E. Lefton, and Manual Sherberg, published by Wiley Interscience.
- *Selling: A Behavioral Science Approach,* by Joseph W. Thompson, published by McGraw-Hill Book Company.

- *Salesmanship: Modern Viewpoints on Personal Communication,* by Steven J. Shaw and Joseph W. Thompson, published by Holt, Rinehart and Winston, Inc.
- *Professional Salesmanship,* by Kenneth B. Haas, published by Holt, Rinehart and Winston, Inc.

These books deal with selling. For the even more complicated skill of training salespeople, see *Handbook of Sales Training,* written by the National Society of Sales Training Executives, published by McGraw-Hill Book Company.

24 Supervision

The rules of good supervision, like the Ten Commandments, are all very familiar—but difficult to apply.

Some of the most important ones are:

1. The example you set is more important than the policies you preach. If you come in late now and then, do not expect your employees to be any more punctual.
2. The Golden Rule of good management is: Take a real, personal interest in each of your staff members. Know them as individuals—their interests, their ambitions, their hobbies, their worries.
3. Make sure that all individuals know what is expected of them, how well they are measuring up to those expectations, and what they can do about it if they are not.
4. Be fair and impartial. Every rule must be applied with equal severity or equal leniency to everyone on the staff.
5. If an employee consistently fails to do something he or she should do, ask yourself these questions:
   a. Does the employee know he or she should do it?
   b. Does the employee know why it is important to do it?
   c. Does the employee know how to do it?
   d. Does the employee know why it is to his or her personal advantage to do it?

THE IMPORTANCE OF FEEDBACK

As we saw in Chapter 19 on "Motivation," Dr. B. F. Skinner has found that we can shape behavior by giving prompt feedback. The application of this principle to the office environment is that the manager lets everybody know, as immediately and as frequently as is practical, the answer to the question "How'm I doin'?"

This can be in the form of reports, scores, achievement of objectives, pats on the back, or anything else that keeps saying, "You did it right that time!"

Office manager, ask yourself: Does everybody in your office know, as rapidly as possible (and without piling up a lot of paperwork and reports), how well each job is being handled?

DISCIPLINE

What about the people who simply will not arrive on time, will not keep their desks clean, will not adhere to some other aspect of office policy? Most experienced managers agree that the most effective disciplinary steps are:

1. Never criticize the employee in front of fellow employees. Get the offender aside.

2. Explain why it is important that the policy be observed. In what way does it interfere with efficiency or morale if one employee consistently breaks it? (If it has no effect on office efficiency or customer relations, are you sure the regulation is necessary?)

3. If the offense is committed a second time, again explain to the employee the importance of playing by the rules and caution the employee that repeated instances will result in disciplinary action.

4. On the third offense, if it is important enough, tell the employee *in writing* that a repetition will result in a temporary suspension, a discharge, or whatever the penalty may be.

5. If it is necessary to take disciplinary action, tell the employee but also put it in writing.

Keep these statements in your files; you may need them if the person you discipline files some sort of discrimination charge against you.

SETTING PERFORMANCE STANDARDS

There are a number of obvious advantages to being able to provide objective measurements of employee productivity. Among them are:

1. Employees are motivated by a sense of achievement when they meet or exceed expectations.
2. Appraisal interviews and salary administration are based on accepted facts rather than opinions or emotions.
3. The measurements can form the basis of an incentive bonus system.
4. The manager can measure the overall increases in office productivity.

In short, such measurements answer the employee's frequently felt but often unvoiced question: "How'm I doing?"

There are three possible ways of establishing productivity standards.

Productivity Measurements

In some cases it is possible to establish statistical measurements of the "normal" or "medium" output. If a number of people are doing the same measurable task, it is simply a question of counting. Use the method used in scoring diving contests when there are a number of judges: cross out the highest score and the lowest score, and get the average of the rest. This then is the norm we expect everyone to attain.

It should be stressed that this is the "floor," not the "ceiling." This is the *least* we expect. Performance below the norm is unacceptable. Productivity above the norm is encouraged by all the factors mentioned in the chapter on motivation.

This type of measurement is not always possible in a small office, where there are only a few employees and not many of the outputs are measurable, but it can sometimes be used. Even if only one or two people are doing a "countable" task, one can take counts on successive days and arrive at a norm.

As in all instances when you observe or measure employee performance, be sure the employees understand that the goal is to make the flow of work more efficient, and therefore easier and more pleasant.

Performance Standards

Another approach is to take each function listed in the job description and complete this statement:

"This part of the job is being done satisfactorily when ____________."
Fill in the blank with some objective, measurable description of the conditions that will exist when the job is done right.

For example, if one function in a job description is "Open and distribute mail," the performance standard might be: "This is being handled satisfactorily when all mail has been delivered to the proper persons within a half-hour after its arrival in the office, and not more than two items of mail per month are delivered to the wrong person or department."

It is a good management practice to explain to the employees why these standards will be of value both to them and to the company, and then let them participate in setting the standards. In many cases they will tend to set standards that are too high rather than too low.

Management by Objectives

This is a management technique that is really based on common sense, in that all of us tend to use it to some extent, although often not as well as we might.

In MBO, as it is commonly called, the owner or top manager sits down before the beginning of a year and lists all the objectives he or she wishes to accomplish in the coming year. Each objective should be observable and measurable.

The owner, for example, will set objectives like "X" amount in sales volume, "Y" amount of costs, "Z" amount of net profit, "P" number of new products or services developed, "Q" increase in market share. These annual goals are broken down into quarterly goals, seasonally adjusted if need be.

Then each department head reporting to the owner draws up a set of objectives which that department must attain if the company is to achieve its overall objectives.

The sales manager, for example, will have the same "X" sales volume as the target, but will have others such as: hire and develop "Y" new salespeople, hold direct sales costs to "Z" dollars and indirect sales costs to "P" dollars, add "Q" number of new customers, and so on.

Subordinates reporting to the sales manager draw up their own objectives for their territories and departments, and so on down the line.

Each executive sits down with each subordinate every quarter to review progress toward the objectives and to determine what steps must be taken if one or more of them are not being achieved.

25 The Appraisal Interview

As was mentioned briefly in Chapter 19, an important element in keeping employees both motivated and productive is for their manager to sit down with them individually at regular intervals and answer the questions that are so important to them: "How am I doing? What does the company think of me? What should I be doing differently?" This process is called "appraisal and counseling" or simply "the appraisal interview."

Your company may have a formal appraisal procedure. If so, this chapter will help you use it more effectively. But even if your company does not have one, or if you are an independent office manager, it will pay you to develop your own appraisal system.

The appraisal interview, properly conducted, will help you to:

1. Keep employees motivated.
2. Increase their productivity.
3. Keep valuable employees and reduce turnover.
4. Maintain good employee relationships.
5. Prepare capable employees for promotion.
6. Delegate some of your tasks to subordinates.
7. Determine who should get merit increases in salary.

The appraisal interview, briefly consists of your sitting down with each person who reports to you, someplace where there is privacy and will be no interruptions, and reviewing with the employee what portions of the job are being handled well, what portions need improvement, and how the employee can make those improvements.

In a larger office, where your subordinates have people working under them, you conduct appraisal interviews with the people who report directly to you, and they do the appraisals of the people who report to them.

How often should the appraisal interview be held? With a new employee you may want to do it once a quarter. With established employees, once every year or once every six months is usual. But whatever frequency you adopt, hold the appraisal interviews on a regular schedule. This function is too important to be pushed aside by other demands on your time.

Should you discuss salary increases during appraisal interviews? This subject was discussed briefly in Chapter 20. Most experienced managers advise against it. Discuss salary adjustments at another time. If you try to review performance and discuss salary in the same interview, you have two choices:

1. You discuss salary first, in which case the employee spends the rest of the interview thinking about the new salary instead of hearing what you are saying, or

2. you hold the salary discussion until last, in which case the employee is just waiting to hear how big the raise will be instead of paying attention to the discussion of job performance.

If, during the appraisal interview, the employee asks, "Well, if I'm doing that well, what about a raise?," you can postpone that discussion by saying, "I plan to hold salary review discussions with all of you during the week of such-and-such; in this conversation today, let's confine ourselves to a discussion of your work and the progress you're making."

PREPARING FOR THE INTERVIEW

To be effective, the appraisal must be based on objective performance standards that have previously been discussed with the employees and agreed upon or at least understood by them.

Many of the appraisal procedures used by large corporations require the manager to evaluate the employee on such factors as "initiative," "company loyalty," and "cooperativeness." This type of evaluation puts the manager in an embarrassing situation. How do you measure "initiative"? If an employee rates 75% on "initiative," is that satisfactory? What if the manager gives an employee a low rating on one of these factors, and the employee does not agree with the rating? This would undermine the whole purpose of the appraisal session.

The way to avoid these dead ends is to base appraisal as completely as possible on standards or objectives that are measurable, or at least observable. If your company has a fixed form for you to fill out with some of those "brave," "clean," "loyal," and "reverent" ratings, go ahead and fill it out to keep the Personnel Department happy, but stress measurable performance in your conversation with the employee.

What this means is that if you have not provided clear job descriptions and set some goals or standards for your employees, you are really not ready to conduct appraisal interviews. Work out the performance standards with your people, get their agreement on them, and hold your first appraisal interview 3 months after that.

Conducting an effective interview is much easier if you use some kind of appraisal form. A suggested form appears in Figure 25-1. Modify it as required to suit your needs, then run off a supply of copies.

Whether or not you use a form like that in Figure 25-1, preparation for the appraisal interview consists of these steps:

1. Collect all the necessary information about the employee's performance. This would include any statistics on job output, records of your previous appraisal interviews, and any notes you have made as to the employee's strengths, weaknesses, and development needs.

2. Decide upon the two or three functions the employee is performing best and the two or three where improvement is needed. Do not try to work on more than three functions at this interview; if there are more weaknesses, concentrate on three now and postpone the rest until later.

3. Think tentatively about what sort of action plan you feel will be needed. But do not write this on the form; the final plan will be worked out by you and the employee during the interview.

Some companies have the employee, as well as the manager, fill out some kind of appraisal form before the interview. During the interview they compare the two ratings and discuss reasons for any differences.

CONDUCTING THE INTERVIEW

Set the Stage

Very few people relish the thought of having their performance evaluated. To some, the thought of an appraisal interview may be rather terrifying. So it is important to put the employee at ease.

Explain (if it is the first time) or remind the employee (in later interviews) that the whole purpose of the interview is to discuss the employee's progress; answer any questions; and jointly work out ways of helping the employee overcome any weaknesses, develop abilities, and (if appropriate) qualify for promotion.

A minute or two of chitchat about current events of mutual interest often helps to create a relaxed atmosphere. Encourage the employee to talk. Ask how he or she feels about the job or if there are any questions.

"Reinforce" the Strengths

As psychologist B. F. Skinner learned through experiments with both animals and people, we can "shape" behavior by giving people "positive reinforcement" when they do what we want them to do. "Positive reinforcement" can ultimately include such things as raises, promotions, and awards. But in this interview you give positive reinforcement by congratulating the employee on those parts of the job in which performance is above the expected standards or goals.

Tip: No not dish out all your compliments at the start of the interview. Save a few to bring up later on.

Get Agreement on Weaknesses

Getting agreement is important. If the employee does not agree that performance is below standard in the area you are discussing, the employee will not believe in the need for improvement and will not pay much attention to the action plan.

Ask about the causes of any substandard performance. There may be conditions over which the employee has no control.

What if the employee has some serious emotional or physical problem, such as alcoholism, drug addiction, or marital conflict? Do not try to solve the problem yourself; that is a task for a professional. But perhaps you can refer the employee to professional help, either within or outside of the company.

Summarize the Evaluation and Get Agreement

This need not be a long summary. Just hit the highlights of the outstanding and below par performances—and make sure the employee agrees. Instead of merely asking "Do you agree?" and getting a perfunctory "Yes," ask an open-ended question to get feedback: "Mary, let's summarize what we've been talking about. What would you agree are the areas where we'll work to get improvement?"

APPRAISAL FORM Date ____________

Employee ______________________ Position ______________________

Length of service ________________ Time in present job ____________

NOTE: The purpose of this appraisal is to improve this individual's performance in the current position. Promotions and salary increases are not treated in this form and should not be discussed during the performance appraisal interview.

SECTION 1. Appraisal of job functions

Instructions: Rate the individual's performance for each job function in terms of the agreed standards. The ratings are: BS = Below Standard; MS = Meets Standard, and ES = Exceeds Standard. Under "Comments" enter any specifics, good or bad, that influenced your rating. If on a particular function there are no standards or you have insufficient information to make an honest rating, do not rate that function; explain briefly under "Comments."

Job Function ______________

Standards	BS	MS	ES

Comments ______________________________________

Job Function ______________

Standards	BS	MS	ES

Comments ______________________________________

Job Function ______________

Standards	BS	MS	ES

Comments ______________________________________

Job Function ______________

Standards	BS	MS	ES

Comments ______________________________________

Figure 25-1
Sample Appraisal Form

SECTION II. Summary

Overall performance rating.

Check the box opposite the paragraph that most nearly describes your evaluation.

☐ Exceeds standards; performs above normal expectations.

☐ Meets standards; performs as expected.

☐ Below standards; needs help to bring performance up to standards.

Strengths

What part of the job does the individual do best? Limit your list to three major job functions.

Areas in need of improvement

In what areas of the job does the individual need the most improvement? List not more than three specific job functions or activities.

Past year's development objectives	How well was each accomplished?

SECTION III. Action Plan

This plan commits the manager and the employee to a course of action. It is to be decided upon as a joint project during the appraisal interview.

Development objective	Specific actions to be taken by employee	Responsibility of manager	Target date
1.			
2.			
3.			
4.			

Planned by ______________________ and ______________________

(manager's signature) (employee's signature)

Figure 25-1 (continued)

Develop an Action Plan

Although you may have had a preliminary course of action in mind before the interview even starts, at this stage of the conversation the two of you jointly agree upon an action plan.

What should the employee do? Write it down. What can you, as the manager, do? Write that down too. This shows that you are making a commitment as well as asking for one. You are helping, not just criticizing.

The action plan should be specific, measurable, and challenging. Agree on a target date for accomplishing each part of the plan.

You may or may not want to go through the formality of having both of you sign the action plan.

Follow Up on the Plan

This is critical. It shows the employee that you are dedicated to the program and were not just "going through the motions" during the appraisal interview. Put dates on your calendar if necessary to remind yourself to check with the employee and see how the plan is working.

PREREQUISITES FOR SUCCESSFUL APPRAISAL INTERVIEWS

As you gain more experience in conducting appraisal interviews, occasionally review the "prerequisites" and "barriers" listed below. This will help you make them even more effective.

The prerequisites for a successful interview are:

1. A relationship of trust between the employee and manager
2. A conviction on the part of the subordinate that the manager really cares
3. The ability of the two people to communicate
4. The willingness on the manager's part to take enough time to prepare for and conduct the interview

BARRIERS TO SUCCESSFUL INTERVIEWS

1. Thinking of the entire process as essentially a disciplinary device
2. Not finding the time—or not finding enough time
3. Going into the session with preconceived ideas about what is causing the problem and what should be done about it
4. Being too preoccupied with day-to-day affairs to give the process your complete concentration
5. Doing too much of the talking yourself

Index